ABYSS OF DESPAIR

(YEVEN METZULAH)

JUDAICA SERIES

William B. Helmreich, series editor

The goal of this series is to make available social science works in the field of Jewish studies that are recognized as having made a lasting contribution to both. Some of these books have been out of print for decades, others for only a short period. What they have in common is the recognition by scholars in the field that they deserve to be made accessible to a wider public as well as to experts in the discipline.

ABYSS OF DESPAIR
(YEVEN METZULAH)

The Famous 17th Century Chronicle Depicting Jewish Life in Russia and Poland During the Chmielnicki Massacres of 1648-1649

NATHAN HANOVER

Translated from the Hebrew by
ABRAHAM J. MESCH

With a New Foreword by
WILLIAM B. HELMREICH

Transaction Publishers
New Brunswick (U.S.A.) and London (U.K.)

Sixth printing 2009
New material this edition © 1983 by Transaction Publishers, New Brunswick, New Jersey.
 Original edition © 1950 by Abraham J. Mesch. Published by Bloch Publishing Co.

All rights reserved under International and Pan-American Copyright Conventions. No part of this book may be reproduced or transmitted in any form or by any means, electronic or mechanical, including photocopy, recording, or any information storage and retrieval system, without prior permission in writing from the publisher. All inquiries should be addressed to Transaction Publishers, Rutgers—The State University, 35 Berrue Circle, Piscataway, New Jersey 08854-8042. www.transactionpub.com

This book is printed on acid-free paper that meets the American National Standard for Permanence of Paper for Printed Library Materials.

Library of Congress Catalog Number: 82-19242
ISBN: 978-0-87855-927-5
Printed in the United States of America

Library of Congress Cataloging-in-Publication Data Hanover, Nathan Nata, d. 1683.
    Abyss of despair-Yeven metzulah.
    Translation of: Yeven metzulah.
    Reprint. Originally published: New York : Bloch Pub. Co., 1950.
        1. Gezerottahve-tat, 1648-1649.   2. Jews—Poland—persecutions.   . Jews—Ukraine—Persecutions.   4. Khmel'nyts'kyĭ Bohdan, ca. 1594-1657.   5. Poland—Ethnic relations.   6. Ukraine—Ethnic relations.   I. Mesch, Abraham J.   II. Title.
    III. Title: Yeven metzulah.

DS135.P6H313   1983   947'.71004924   82-19242
ISBN: 0-87855-927-2

CONTENTS

Illustrations vii
Translator's Note ix
Foreword to the Transaction Edition xi
Translator's Introduction 1
The Life and Work of Nathan Hanover 13
Author's Introduction 23
    I.   Abyss of Despair 27
    II.   The Massacres of Nalevaiko 29
    III. The Massacres of Pawliuk 31
    IV. The Brutal Oppressions of Chmiel 34
    V.   The Massacres of Nemirow 50
    VI. The Massacres of Tulczyn 54
    VII. The Massacres by Polannoe 62
    VIII. The Massacres of Ostrog and Zaslaw 70
    IX. The Massacres of Konstantynow 72
    X.   The Massacres of Lithuania 78
    XI. The Massacres of Bar 80
    XII. The Massacres of Lwow 83
    XIII. The Massacres of Narol 87
    XIV. The Massacres of Zamosc 89
    XV. The Second Massacre of Ostrog 95
    XVI. The Inner Life of the Jews in the
           Kingdom of Poland 110
    XVII. Notes 122

ILLUSTRATIONS

	FACING PAGE
Map. Poland and Lithuania in 1564	1
Traditional Drawing of the Maharsha	13
Bogdan Chmielnicki	27
Synagogue in Zolkiew	85
Synagogue in Szaragrod	85
Typical Clothes of Polish Jews During 16th and 17th Centuries	110

TRANSLATOR'S NOTE

The translation of Rabbi Nathan Hanover's "Yeven Metzulah" was undertaken some two years ago and its publication was to coincide with the 300th anniversary of the Chmielnicki Massacres of 1648–49. Numerous interruptions, however, prevented me from completing the work sooner.

In rendering Hanover's chronicle into English I aimed primarily at reproducing his text as closely to the original as possible. I made no attempts to edit or alter its phraseology except where clarity of expression demanded it. I endeavored to retain the flavor of Hanover's simple rabbinic style. The biblical idiom is characteristic of Hanover's writing. His narrative, therefore, is replete with phrases, verses and sometimes complete passages from the Scriptures. The reader will readily find reference to these in the notes at the end of the book.

Several editions of the "Yeven Metzulah" were used as the basis for the translation. The vocalized edition by Israel Hailpern (Hakibutz Hameuchad, Israel 1945) and the Klal edition (Berlin 1923) were most frequently consulted. For the biographical sketch of Nathan Hanover I relied considerably on the pioneer work by J. Israelsohn in Jacob Shatzky's "Gezeroth Tach" (Yivo, Vilna, 1938). For the translation of the biblical passages I made use of the Jewish Publication Society edition of the Holy Scriptures except, in rare instances, where other translations were consulted.

TRANSLATOR'S NOTE

In preparing this work for press I was fortunate to have had the learned counsel of a number of friends and colleagues. I am deeply grateful to them. Dr. Judah Rosenthal, Librarian of the College of Jewish Studies, Chicago, Ill. has been exceedingly helpful and encouraging. I am indebted to him for much assistance. I am grateful to Rabbi Leonard C. Mishkin, Educational Director of the Associated Talmud Torahs of Chicago, for suggesting the work and for offering many valuable comments. Many thanks to Dr. Solomon Grayzel, Editor of the Jewish Publication Society of America, for reading the manuscript and for offering pertinent suggestions from which, I am sure, the book benefited, and for contributing the preface. My appreciation is also extended to my secretary, Henne Lee Seligman, for her gracious cooperation in typing the manuscript.

Finally, I wish to express my thanks and appreciation to the following members of my community whose generosity made the publication of this book possible: Frank A. Abelson (In Memoriam), Jacob Allen, A. C. Berman, Robert Berman, Sol Berman, Ed Greenberg, Max Greenwald, Dr. I. Z. Harris, Max and Harry Hurvich, Max L. Kimerling, Bernard Lewis, Joe and Hannah Levy (Atlanta, Ga.), Louis Pizitz, Philip Randman, Mrs. J. Rotenstreich, Joseph Smolian and Joseph Solomon.

A. J. M.

Birmingham, Ala.
December 1949
Kislev 5710

FOREWORD TO THE TRANSACTION EDITION

Abyss of Despair is an extremely important book. Written by a Jewish scholar-traveler who was there, it is a graphic and gripping account of one of the worst catastrophes ever to befall the Jewish people. In the period 1648-1658, tens of thousands of Jews perished in Poland and in the Ukraine. Rabbi Nathan Hanover describes the events themseves and how they affected the Jewish community, and his chronicle deserves attention on its historical merits alone. There are also other reasons why an understanding of those times is crucial.

The period immediately preceding the Chmielnicki massacres was one in which the Jews enjoyed relative peace and prosperity. Many were employed as overseers and tax collectors for the Polish nobles. In this capacity, they were required to collect rent and taxes from the impoverished Ukrainian peasantry and some have argued that this explains the severity of the anti-Jewish attacks. On the other hand, no historical documents have ever been presented in support of the idea that the Jews exploited the peasants. Of course, the Jews may have been resented simply because of their role, but this must be understood in its proper context. The Jews were compelled to engage in certain occupations because their opportunities for earning a living were restricted to these areas. Hanover's account demonstrates how the Jews were caught in the middle of a set of unfortunate circumstances. Not only were the Ukrainians their enemies but the Poles also viewed them as expendable, and they often betrayed them.

In terms of numbers, the Chmielnicki massacres rank as one of the greatest calamities ever to befall the Jewish people. Perhaps 10 percent of the population was wiped out, entire communities were destroyed, and the course of Jewish history was fundamentally altered. The era prior to 1648 was a golden one in terms of Jewish culture. Institutions of learning flourished, and Poland was a renowned world center of scholarship. The Polish government was generally tolerant toward the Jews and allowed them a good deal of autonomy in their internal affairs. All this changed in 1648, and the magnitude of the destruction caused the Jewish community to turn inward. Messianic movements, the best known of which was that led by Sabbatai Zevi, gained converts among Polish Jews desperate to find both an explanation and a solution for their suffering. Many believed that the decimation of their ranks was a sign that the arrival of the Messiah was imminent.

It is almost a truism that catastrophic events often have beneficial results. The Chmielnicki programs were, in part, responsible for the development of a climate conducive to the emergence of Hasidism. Without going into great detail, Hasidism arose in the eighteenth century as a response to the thousands of Eastern European Jews who felt alienated because they were not well versed in Talmudic learning. Led by the Baal Shem Tov, its founder, Hasidism argued that scholarship was not the only way to achieve closeness to God. God was everywhere, said the Hasidim, and could be reached through prayer, song, and dance.

The appeal of this movement to the Jewish masses was successful, in large measure, because the previous century had witnessed the destruction of the centers of Jewish learning. The dearth of leadership and the lack of adequate schools to transmit the tradition, meant that the community was susceptible to approaches that did not require great knowledge and erudition. In time, however, Hasidism came to be seen as a major contribution to Jewish religious thought and not simply as a folk movement.

In addition to Messianism and Hasidism, the pogroms had

an effect on Jewish migration. From the eleventh to the fifteenth century Jews had moved eastward. After 1648, this pattern reversed itself as hundreds of thousands fled the Cossack terror. Although such migration ebbed and flowed during the next three centuries, the ultimate effect was the redistribution of world Jewry to the point where Western Europe became a major center once again. As a result, Jews were living in France, Germany, and Austria, when the Enlightenment swept through that part of the world. One can only speculate on the course of history had men like Karl Marx, Sigmund Freud, Claude Lévi-Strauss, Albert Einstein, and thousands of others been confined to life in the *shtetls* of Eastern Europe.

In an era when so much has been written on the Nazi holocaust, it is important to recognize that this last tragedy dwarfs all previous holocausts only in magnitude but not in kind, and that the brutality of Chmielnicki made the work of the Nazis that much easier. It is no accident that Eastern Europe was the location for most of the major concentration camps. The Ukrainians in particular tended to cooperate with the Nazis in their efforts to exterminate the Jews. Thus Babi Yar became synonymous with the desire to forget and to cover up. Books like *Abyss of Despair* are valuable because they do not allow us to forget. As we read Hanover's description of the atrocities committed by Chmielnicki and his hordes, it becomes clear that Hitler's torture chambers were only technological refinement—the precedent had already been set:

> Some were skinned alive and their flesh was thrown to the dogs; some had their hands and limbs chopped off, and their bodies thrown on the highway only to be trampled by wagons and crushed by horses.... The enemy slaughtered infants in the laps of their mothers. They were sliced into pieces like fish. They slashed the bellies of pregnant women, removed their infants and tossed them in their faces. Some women had their

bellies torn open and live cats placed in them. The bellies were then sewed up with the live cats remaining within. They chopped off the hands of the victims so that they would not be able to remove the cats from the bellies.... Some children were pierced with spears, roasted on the fire and then brought to their mothers to be eaten. There was no cruel device of murder in the whole world that was not perpetrated by the enemies.

The most recent oppressor of the Jews is the Soviet Union, and its policies become more understandable when viewed from a historical perspective. Anti-Semitism has always been a part of Russian life and culture, and nowhere has its presence been more noticeable than in the Ukraine where Chmielnicki is still regarded as a national hero. Two hundred thousand Jews were killed in the Ukraine during the Russian Revolution. Figures released for the years 1960-1963 provide further confirmation: fifty-five percent of those sentenced to death throughout the Soviet Union in those years were Jews, while in the Ukraine, where Jews constituted but 2 percent of the population, 90 percent of those sentenced to death were Jews.

Those who are tempted to believe the current Soviet line about the presumed distinction between anti-Zionism and anti-Semitism would do well to read *Abyss of Despair*. Those who romanticize *shtetl* culture would find in Hanover's account grim evidence of the historical relationships between the Jews and the Gentiles who populated the thousands of hamlets and villages that dotted the Eastern European landscape—each with its own different yet similar story to tell. At the same time, a careful reading of these events and an examination of the larger historical framework in which they occurred, ought to provide hope that human beings can, if they have the will, find ways to transcend tragedy and misfortune, rebuild their lives, and develop new and perhaps more powerful ways to ex-

FOREWORD TO THE TRANSACTION EDITION

press the essence of their heritage and culture. That, in the larger sense, is the true message of this book.

William B. Helmreich
City University, New York

Courtesy, The Jewish Publication Society of America

INTRODUCTION

The years 1948–49 mark the 300th anniversary of the dreadful Chmielnicki Massacres in Poland and the Ukraine, known as *Gezeroth Tach Vetat*. The pogroms which began in the spring of 1648 and which continued for several years claimed the lives of hundreds of thousands of Jews and the devastation of hundreds of communities and settlements.[1] The period was one of the bloodiest in Jewish history. The fury of the slaughter, the unbridled cruelty, the unspeakable atrocities of the insurgents made the horrors of earlier days pale into insignificance. Only the recent extermination of European Jewry by the Nazis surpassed that in Poland of three hundred years ago.

The Jews of Poland lived rather tranquilly and securely prior to the outbreak of the hostilities. They enjoyed comparative autonomy and peace. Polish Jewry was well integrated, and its institutions flourished. Many Jews had been employed as overseers, administrators and tax farmers by the wealthy Polish landowners. It was the task of the Jewish tax farmer to keep his master supplied with the necessary funds. This could be achieved only by taxing the peasants heavily and by increasing the burden of their labors. Gradually the Jews became the virtual masters of the peasants and the sole administrators of the large estates.

The oppressive measures usually employed by the landowner had to be employed by his Jewish lessee. The continuous demand for money by his employer forced the Jew to appear as the peasants' tyrant and oppressor. In reality, however, he was only carrying out the bidding of his master, the Pan. Thus contemporary historians relate that the Pans would levy a tax for the baptism of each peasant child, for the marriage of each peasant daughter, for the burying of their dead.[2] These levies were collected by the Jewish stewards and delivered to the landlord.[3]

A strong animosity also existed between the bulk of the people of the Ukraine whose religion was overwhelmingly Greek Catholic and the Poles who were Roman Catholics. Thus the hatred which the peasants bore against their masters was caused not only by economic oppression but also by religious differences. They looked upon their Polish oppressors not only as tyrants but also as infidels, and upon the Jew, as infidel and tyrant, and also as the master's tool.

It is no wonder then that under such conditions the attitude of the peasants toward the Jew was not a favorable one, to say the least. Even though they were fully aware that the Jew was merely an agent for the landowner, the peasants could not but feel hatred towards him. The situation was intolerable and filled with ominous forebodings.

The impending catastrophe, however, received impetus from another source. The Cossacks in South Russia had always been a source of irritation to the Kingdom of Poland. They were a warlike group who

INTRODUCTION

lived in the Ukrainian Steppes bordering Crimea. They frequently attacked caravans of merchants headed for Crimea and points east. They consisted of a motley of diversified nationalities and religions. In due time they developed a sense of unity among themselves and became, so to speak, Ukrainian nationals. The Crimean Tartars, too, often attacked the eastern provinces of Poland and looted their settlements. The Polish government, therefore, encouraged the Cossacks to organize themselves into bands for the purpose of protecting the borders of the kingdom. Thus the Cossacks served a double purpose; they defended the southeastern border against the marauding Crimeans and at the same time forsook their banditry which had been of deep concern to the government. They organized themselves into divisions, each one numbering a thousand, and each headed by a captain. Their commander-in-chief was known as the Hetman [4] who was appointed by the King himself. Thus the erstwhile robbers received national recognition. Special privileges were conferred upon them, and some were honored with titles of nobility.[5] This encouraged many riff-raff to join them. The Polish government, however, could not accommodate all of them into the Cossack divisions. Hence, two types of Cossacks came into being; those registered in the service of Poland and the unregistered who lived in a so called no-man's land beyond the Dnieper Falls known as Zaporozhe.[6] They maintained themselves mainly from piracy on the Black Sea, robbery, fishing and hunting. Frequently, the Polish government sought to convert these Cossacks into farmers but they preferred the life of adventure. They rebelled against governmental edicts only to be suppressed by force. At times the Cossacks appealed to the Ukrainian peasants to join them in their rebellion but they did not respond. Those who did join suffered retribution when the rebellion failed. Obsequious and penitent they would ask forgiveness from the Polish government. It happened frequently that the registered Cossacks in the service of the government joined the others in rebellion against the Kingdom of Poland. Their punishment was to have their number reduced to a minimum while the rest were forced to till the soil.

Deprived of their privileges and military standing, angered and disappointed, the Cossacks in the Ukraine were in a continuous state of rebellion. They were looking for a leader who would initiate the revolt against Poland. Such a leader appeared in the person of Bogdan Chmielnicki.

Chmielnicki's place of residence was Chigirin. He was the son of a wealthy landowner and received a fairly good education. He participated with his father in a war in Wallachia where the elder Chmielnicki was killed while the son became a prisoner of the Tartars. After two years of imprisonment he was ransomed and returned home to become heir to his father's estate. He considered himself a loyal subject of Poland and never joined the sporadic Cossack uprisings.

In 1639 Daniel Czaplinski became assistant governor of Chigirin, a position formerly occupied by Chmielnicki's father. Both Chmielnicki and Czaplin-

INTRODUCTION

ski were widowers. A quarrel resulted between them over a comely young maiden, Helena, whose hand both sought. Chmielnicki, however, emerged the victor in this rivalry. The disappointed Czaplinski then attacked Chmielnicki's estate, seized a good portion of his property, and also the beautiful Helena. Chmielnicki appealed to the Polish government but received no satisfaction. He appeared personally before King Wladislaw IV and the king granted him an official document establishing his right to the estate, but upon his return to claim it, he found that Czaplinski had, in the interim, appropriated his entire estate and also married his beloved Helena.

The clash with Czaplinski, the loss of his estate, and the marriage of his beloved to his rival left him embittered and filled his heart with vengeance. Chmielnicki was now prepared to join other Cossack leaders in a revolt against the Kingdom of Poland. Apparently, the plan that such a revolt was in preparation reached the governor Koniecpolski and Bogdan was imprisoned. He denied the accusation that he was plotting against the government and was released in the custody of the Cossack officer, Kriczewski, who was a personal friend of Chmielnicki. No sooner did Chmielnicki breathe the air of freedom than his friend permitted him to escape to Zaporozhe, beyond the Dnieper Falls.

It was there that Chmielnicki called upon the Cossacks to rise against the Polish oppressors and to enlist the help of the general Ukrainian populace in the effort to throw off the yoke of Poland and of the Jews. Chmielnicki was elected the Hetman of the Cossacks and proceeded to conclude an alliance with the Khan of Crimea. The Khan promised to send a large number of Tartar troops to aid the Cossacks in their rebellion.

Chmielnicki's offensive started in April of 1648. He left his camp beyond the Dnieper Falls and moved to the borders of the Ukraine to attack the Polish army. With a combined force of Cossack and Tartar troops he engaged a small force of the Polish army and defeated it. Ten days later he engaged a larger Polish army under the leadership of Mikolai Potocki, near Korsun, and was again victorious. The two victories made a deep impression upon all of the Ukraine. The confidence in the invincibility of Poland was shattered and skepticism regarding the strength of the Cossacks disappeared. The defeat of the Polish armies served as a signal to all the Ukrainian peasants and villagers to leave their homes and join the Cossacks and the Tartars in the rebellion and avenge themselves on the Poles and the Jews. The Cossack rebellion was turned into a general national uprising against the Kingdom of Poland.

Mad with lust for blood Chmielnicki and his hordes attacked the estates of the Pans and devastated them, killing the Jewish administrators. Thus in the towns of Pereyaslav, Piratin, Lochwitz and Lubny thousands of Jews were brutally murdered and their property looted. Only those who were willing to join the Greek Orthodox church were spared. Many fled to the camps of the Tartars hoping to save themselves by being sold as slaves and if fortunate enough, to be ransomed by fellow Jews in neighboring Turkey. The Jews of

INTRODUCTION

Poland ran for their lives. They crowded the highways seeking escape from the sword. Many sought shelter in the large and fortified cities but the Chmielnicki hordes followed them and murdered them.

The great tragedy that befell Polish Jewry stirred the Jews of the rest of the world, and united them in the resolve to bring succor to the Chmielnicki victims. Most communities organized special councils for the purpose of ransoming those held captive by the Tartars, and for the resettlement of those who managed to escape. Appropriate penitential prayers and dirges were composed in memory of the martyrs, and a public fast was instituted. Conferences were called together to deal specifically with the problem of the survivors. Each community was asked to contribute to the maximum of its ability to relieve the plight of the victims, among whom were eminent scholars, Rabbis and preachers. A number of these were later elected to serve important communities in Germany, France, Moravia, and others.

Of the few chronicles which recount the events of this tragic period Nathan Hanover's Yeven Metzulah (literally: The Deep Mire) is by far the most popular and the most authentic. While other chroniclers only list the names of the victimized communities and the number of their slain, Hanover attempts to give us an objective account of the events which led to the massacres as well as a realistic description of the bloody attacks. So popular did Hanover's chronicle become that in some communities it was customary to read it annually during the "Three Weeks." [7] Historians like

Heinrich Graetz and others regard his account as reliable and trustworthy.

The Yeven Metzulah is not a dull and monotonous record of ghastly incidents. It is a graphic delineation of a great tragedy that came to pass to an unsuspecting Polish Jewry. Hanover was a gifted historian who knew the intricate workings of history. Thus the reader gleans an understanding of the causes which led to the Cossack uprising and a detailed account of the perpetrations in each community. In order to achieve this aim Hanover begins his tale of woe with the year 1592 when the Poles forced the Greek Orthodox Ukrainians to embrace Roman Catholicism. He records the aborted rebellions of Nalewaiko in 1602 and Pawliuk in 1639,[8] during which many synagogues were destroyed and some two hundred Jews murdered, as the overtures to the Chmielnicki uprising of 1648.

Many historians have attempted to characterize Bogdan Chmielnicki as the national liberator of the oppressed Ukrainian masses, the hero of the downtrodden and the benefactor of the exploited peasants. Hanover, however, pictures him as a ruthless oppressor, a merciless cut-throat and a blood-thirsty tyrant. At each mention of his name he adds the phrase, "May his name be blotted out." Yet, Hanover does not fail to emphasize the miserable plight of the peasants whose suffering at the hands of the Polish nobles may have justified their retaliation. Nor does he absolve the Jews of any guilt when he says: "Even the *lowliest* among them (the Jews) became their overlords." [9]

Hanover was an eye witness to the massacres during

INTRODUCTION

1648. The account of those events shows his personal reaction to them. Information regarding events that occurred in 1649, he collected from new arrivals who fled from the sword of the Cossacks. For at this time he himself had already been a homeless wanderer.

It was from these survivors that he obtained various versions of the massacres. In fact, the report of the massacre in Narol he received, as he states, from a woman who survived the carnage. Hanover also made use of several publications which narrated the events of 1648–49. Chief among these was the Tzok Ha-itim ("Troublous Times") by Meir of Szczebrzeszyn, published in Krakow in 1650. Some historians do not attribute much reliability to a number of incidents related in the Yeven Metzulah. They find them irreconcilable with historical fact. Thus for instance, Hanover tells that two Jews, Zechariah and Jacob Sobilenki, played an important and decisive role in the conflict between Chmielnicki and Alexander Koniecpolski and that the Chmielnicki uprising was a result of Zechariah Sobilenki's betrayal. This story is indeed unlikely. It is hard to believe that the governor had to depend on a Jew's information in order to determine the extent of Chmielnicki's wealth. It is also hard to believe that Chmielnicki sought advice from Jacob Sobilenki as to how to extricate himself from his plight after his imprisonment. Hanover does not touch upon Chmielnicki's conflict with Czaplinski. The story of Helena, the chief source of trouble between the two, seems to have been completely unknown to him. Similarly, the incident with Count

Czwierczinski, who together with his wife and two daughters were murdered by the Cossacks, also seems improbable for it is an historical fact that the Count had no children.[10]

There is definitely a tendency on the part of Hanover to exaggerate when recording the number of both the Polish and the Cossack-Tartar forces. Everywhere he adds, "their number was like the sand on the shores of the sea." Equally doubtful and incorrect are some of his geographical designations. Having lived in Zaslaw, Hanover may not have been sufficiently acquainted with the proximity of the various communities which he discusses.

His sympathetic appraisal of Count Jeremy Wiśniowiecki has also been the object of historical criticism. Hanover portrays the Count as a kind-hearted and noble person, a man who had the interest of the persecuted Jews at heart and who sought to protect them at the risk of his own life. They claim that Wiśniowiecki was representative of the autocratic and imperialistic Polish nobility, and that he was not the benevolent person he describes him to be. However, other chroniclers, such as the author of Tzok-Ha-Itim, also give the same favorable and sympathetic appraisal of the Count.

Many of the stories depicted in the Yeven Metzulah have become classical examples of Jewish heroism. Some of the episodes served as inspiring themes for modern novelists.[11] They are written with dramatic force and skill. The readiness of the young maidens to die for the sanctification of the Name is described with

INTRODUCTION

tenderness and pathos. Some were drowned, others let themselves be stabbed or shot in order not to be defiled. They remained impervious to the offers by the enemy to spare their lives in exchange of baptism. They defied their persecutors and bravely met their fate.

The final chapter of the book is devoted to a detailed description of the social, religious and economic life of Polish Jewry during the 17th century. Here we have a concise but colorful account of Jewish community life; its educational system, its reverence for the scholar, its institutions and organizations. It was a well integrated and peaceful life the Jews of Poland had. Hanover prefaces his description of Polish Jewry with the remark that it was "founded on principles of righteousness and justice."

As a Rabbi and a Kabbalist, Hanover employs a style typical of his day. He was primarily influenced by the style of the Book of Esther. Here and there phrases and sometimes complete verses are lifted out of that book and used appropriately in the Yeven Metzulah.

It is no wonder then that of all the chronicles which tell of the massacres of the Jews, the Yeven Metzulah was the most popular. It was translated into many languages. A Yiddish translation appeared while the author was still alive. Each time the Jew experienced a new wave of persecution, pogroms and massacres, a new edition of the Yeven Metzulah appeared. Thus, following the pogroms of Denikin and Petliura during the first World War, a popular edition of the Yeven Metzulah was published and circulated. As late as nineteen hundred and forty-five, immediately following World War II, "Hakibutz Hameuchad" in Israel published a popular annotated edition of the book by Israel Hailperin with an introduction by the Hebrew poet, Jacob Fichman.

The perusal of the pages of Hanover's chronicle which depicts the tribulation and misery of Polish Jewry in the middle of the seventeenth century, thus served as a source of hope to suffering Jewry in succeeding generations.

Traditional Drawing of the MAHARSHA
(Rabbi Samuel Edels)
Head of the Yeshivah of Ostrog

THE LIFE AND WORK OF NATHAN HANOVER

Nathan Hanover, the author of the chronicle Yeven Metzulah, was born in Ostrog, Volhynia in the early twenties of the seventeenth century. His parents emigrated from Germany to the Ukraine. They probably lived in Hanover because it was a common practice for Jews to adopt the name of the community from which they hailed. It is presumed that they left Hanover at the end of the sixteenth century when all Jews were expelled from that city.

Many Jews emigrated from Germany during the sixteenth century, where they suffered unprecedented persecution and oppression. The Ukraine was especially inviting because the Jews there enjoyed some measure of peace and economic freedom. They were free to travel through the land and pursued their business unmolested. Hanover's family, it can be surmised, left Germany at this time and settled in the Ukraine. We have no information about Hanover's early years. It can be presumed that he received a Jewish education typical of that which he describes in the concluding chapter of his chronicle "Yeven Metzulah." He grew up amidst the scholars and Talmudists of his city and imbibed the teachings of his masters. Ostrog was the great metropolis of Volhynia and had a large Jewish population. It was famous not only as a great business center but even more so as a seat of learning and culture. The most prominent Rabbis and teachers of the age resided there, among them were such great notables as Rabbi Solomon Luria, better known as the Maharshal, Rabbi Samuel Edels, the Maharsha, Rabbi David Halevi, popularly known as the Taz (Ture Zahav), and others.

Nathan's father was evidently a learned man and it is quite possible that he served in the capacity of Rabbi. Nathan frequently refers to him by the title Rabbi. In all likelihood he received his early training from his father and later in the Ostrog Yeshivah which was under the guidance of Maharsha. The study of the Talmud and its commentaries, apparently, was not sufficient to gratify his restless and searching spirit. He, therefore, turned to the Kabbalah and probed into its mystic teachings. He became particularly fascinated by the Lurianic Kabbalah, which had already established itself in Poland and was gradually finding adherents in the Ukraine. The followers of the famous Kabbalist, Isaac Luria Ashkenazi, better known as the Ari, were carrying on a vigorous campaign to spread their master's teachings everywhere. Israel Sarug, and his son-in-law, Solomon Schloemel Dresnitz visited many Jewish communities and sought to indoctrinate the Jews with the Ari's mystic philosophy. Luria's Kabbalah found ready adherents first in Italy and later also in Germany and in Holland whence it penetrated into Poland and where it cultivated enthusiastic supporters. When the Kabbalah spread to the Ukraine, Rabbi Isaiah Horowitz, the author of the Kabbalistic and ethical work Shene Luchoth Haberith, or "Shela," who for a short time served as Rabbi in Ostrog, became one of its chief devotees. Rabbi Samson of Ostropolie, who was martyred in Polannoe during the Chmielnicki revolt, was another of its followers. Nathan Hanover too, became enamoured of this mystic lore, and applied himself diligently to master it. His sermons and Pentateuchal discourses were often based upon Kabbalistic texts and interpretations.

He married the daughter of Abraham of Zaslaw and later removed to reside with his father-in-law. There he occupied himself with preaching. Occasionally he visited other communities and preached to them. Two daughters were born to him in Zaslaw. It is not known whether he had other children. His life during these early years, it can be surmised, was untroubled and peaceful.

The Cossack uprising of 1648 which destroyed so many communities and which almost completely wiped out Ukrainian Jewry brought to an end Nathan's tranquility and caused him to become a wanderer. 1648 was a year of unusual events. It brought peace to central Europe and freedom to England. It was the year in which, according to English millenarians, such as Pierre de la Fons, Jesus was to reappear. It was also the year in which, according to the Zohar, the Messiah was to come. But above all the year 1648 is better known for the rebellion initiated by the Cossack chieftain, Bogdan Chmielnicki which caused untold suffering to the Jewish people.

The city of Zaslaw where Nathan Hanover resided

was devastated by the Cossacks and most of its Jews were murdered. Among the martyred Jews was the father of Nathan, Rabbi Moses Hanover of Ostrog. Nathan fled from the city before it was attacked. After leaving the city of Zaslaw, together with his large family, he started wandering to elude the infuriated Ukrainian mobs. We do not know the circumstances under which he succeeded in his escape from the Cossacks. Hanover, generally, omits personal references in his chronicle which describes these events. He focuses his attention on the whole picture. After making good his escape we find him in Germany where he subsisted on meager earnings from itinerant preaching. Thanks to his oratorical ability and wide range of knowledge he acquired many followers. The sermons preached in Germany during this period he collected into a book called "N'ta Sha-ashuim." This book, however, was never published.

From Germany he proceeded to Holland where he published his sermon "Ta-Ame Succah" which he had preached in Cracow in 1646. He did not remain in Holland very long and proceeded to Italy which had become an important Kabbalah center at that time. Here he hoped to find solace for his troubled soul. The study of Kabbalah was to help him forget the nightmare of the past. Hanover had always been inclined toward asceticism and the impact of the tragic events in Poland drove him closer into the lap of Kabbalistic speculation. Having visited many ravished communities and having talked to the refugees who escaped the carnage, he had accumulated valuable information on

LIFE AND WORK OF HANOVER 17

the Ukrainian massacres. He now had an opportunity to organize his material for publication.

In 1652 we find Hanover in the city of Venice where he published his chronicle "Yeven Metzulah." In 1653 he became the rabbi of Leghorn and spent one year in the Beth Hamidrash of the physician David Valensin, who supported him generously. There he met Hayim Hacohen of Aleppo, a disciple of Rabbi Hayim Vital, the pupil and later successor to Isaac Luria. The two spent much time together studying the Lurianic Kabbalah. Rabbi Hayim Hacohen revealed to him many new and hitherto unpublished teachings of Vital. There he also became acquainted with Nathan Shapira of Jerusalem who was visiting the city and together with him proceeded to Venice where he spent two years in the Yeshivah of the brothers, Abraham and Daniel Mugnon. They befriended and sustained him. In the company of such Kabbalistic exponents as Samuel Abohab, Moses Zacuto and Benjamin Halevi of Safed, he found peace and solitude and devoted himself to diligent studies in mysticism. He received additional material aid from the fellowship "Talmud Torah" of Venice.

After two years in Venice, he proceeded to Wallachia and became Rabbi, first in the city of Jassy and later also in Focsani. The reasons why he left Venice are not known. It is possible that he could not get accustomed to living on charity. The burden of providing for a large family might have impelled him to seek a more profitable occupation elsewhere. He spent a long time in Wallachia and devoted himself to literary endeavors. He succeeded in issuing two works of practical use. One was a dictionary in four languages called "Safa Berurah" (Clear Speech) and the other "Sha-are Zion" (Gates of Zion), an anthology of prayers.

In the '70s of the 17th century, we find him in Ungarisch-Brod, a city in Moravia where he occupied the position of Dayan (Judge) and preacher. His reputation as a Dayan and his excellent sermons gained for him much honor from the members of his community. In this city, too, both of his daughters were married. The fact that he was able to write two books on the Kabbalah during this period shows that he, at last, had attained peace of mind.

Evidently Hanover was not destined to complete his years in tranquility. He who had suffered so much and barely escaped death in the Ukraine had to experience the misery of new massacres. The war between Turkey and Austria had broken out. The turkish army invaded Hungary and proceeded on the way to Vienna. The Hungarian Count, Emeric Tekelli, an avowed enemy of Austria, joined the Turks. Tekelli's army broke into Moravia and the first victim was the city of Brod which was completely without defense. Tekelli's bands attacked the Jews of the city most of whom were at that time gathered in the synagogue for morning prayers. Nathan Hanover was a victim of this attack. His last wish was that he be buried in the Jewish cemetery. His wish was fulfilled. A tombstone bearing his name with appropriate laudatory inscription stands upon his grave.

According to various legends Hanover's burial place

LIFE AND WORK OF HANOVER

is supposed to be in Focsani, Wallachia. Photographs of a tombstone in Focsani, purported to bear his name, are frequently reprinted and claimed to be that of Hanover. However, there is no evidence that the photograph of the tombstone is that of Hanover. The inscription is so worn that the letters can not be deciphered. There is no doubt that Nathan Hanover, having lived the last years of his life in Ungarisch-Brod, was murdered there during the massacre in 1683. The following is the inscription of the tombstone on the cemetery in that city:

"Our holy rabbi, Israel's desire
The sacred vessel, the luminary pure,
The spokesman for Torah was taken by ruthless death
Blessed is he whose soul departed from his chaste body,
Who completed his life by proclaiming the unity of the Creator's Name.
There is none greater than our master, the rabbi Nathan Natta, the son of Moses of Ostrog
His soul ascended on high adorned with the crown of Torah
Twenty days in Tamuz, the month that was turned into mourning and distress
May his soul be bound up in the bond of life."

Thus ended the career of Nathan Hanover. His was a life filled with misery, pain and suffering but also rich and meaningful. His fame was far reaching and his literary achievements are a fitting monument to his memory.

Nathan Hanover wrote many valuable books. Although not a professional historian, he had a realistic approach to history. In his chronicle, "Yeven Metzulah" he appears as an able and competent historian. He was also a linguist and mastered a number of languages, among them Polish, German, Latin and Italian. His linguistic skill is admirably shown by his four language dictionary.

Among the books Hanover wrote, the following may be noted: (1) "Ta-ame Succah," a sermon on the significance of the Feast of Tabernacles and interpretations of the prayers peculiar to the festival. The sermon was delivered in Crakow in 1646 and was published later in Amsterdam in 1652. It contains all Talmudic references pertaining to the festival of Succoth. These Hanover interpreted allegorically. Many of his interpretations are based on the teachings of the Zohar, and show the remarkable influence the Kabbalah had on him in his early years. (2) "Yeven Metzulah," an historic chronicle in which the massacres of 1648–1652 are described. This book was first published in Venice in 1653. It has been translated into French, German, Polish, Russian and Yiddish. (3) "Safa Berurah," a lexicon in four languages, Hebrew, Yiddish, Latin and Italian. The book contains twenty chapters and is divided according to category concepts. The book was of practical benefit to the uprooted Jews of the Ukraine who wandered in countries whose languages were strange to them. It was first published in 1660 in Prague. Another edition appeared in Amsterdam in

LIFE AND WORK OF HANOVER 21

1771 with additions of a column in French. (4) "Sha-are Zion" an anthology of prayers for fasts and feasts, Tikkun Chatzoth, etc. This book is composed of seven chapters. The prayers are of a Kabbalistic nature. They were mostly composed by the disciples of Luria. It became a popular prayer book for the Jews of his time. Many of the prayers have also been included in the prayer books still in use today. The prayer, Ribbono Shel Olam, recited prior to the removal of the Torah from the Ark and the Yehi Ratzon, following the priestly benediction are taken from Hanover's anthology.

Sha-are-Zion was first published in Prague in 1662.

Nathan Hanover had also written a number of works which were not published. His collection of sermons on the Pentateuch and festivals known as "Neta Shaa-shuim" which is mentioned in his introduction to the "Yeven Metzulah" was never published. Neta Ne-eman, a commentary on the teachings of Rabbi Isaac Luria, remained in manuscript. Another book which never saw the light of publication was Tokef Yayin, a Kabbalistic interpretation of the festival of Purim. Also "Yefe Nof," a commentary on the book of psalms based on the Kabbalah was not published.

It is indeed amazing that despite his being exposed to continuous misfortune, aimless wandering and insecurity, Nathan Hanover managed to accumulate such an imposing literary output. One is impressed by his strength of character and profound faith which kept him from disintegrating in the face of all his misery. He, no doubt, found consolation in dedicating himself to these spiritual tasks. Despite his rich literary legacy, however, he is known best for his chronicle, "Yeven Metzulah."

AUTHOR'S INTRODUCTION

"I am the man that hath seen the affliction by the rod of His wrath,"[1] when God smote His people Israel, His first-born. From heaven unto earth He cast down the beautiful and glorious land of Poland, "oh fair in situation, the joy of the whole earth."[2] "The Lord hath swallowed up unsparingly the habitations of Jacob,"[3] the lot of His inheritance,[4] and hath not remembered His footstool in the day of His anger.[5]

All this was foreseen by King David (peace be unto him), when he prophesied the joining of the Tartars and the Greeks[6] to destroy His chosen Israel, in the year ZOTH[7] of the era of creation. The "Greeks," in their typical manner, offered the following ultimatum to the Jews: He that wishes to remain alive must change his faith and publicly renounce Israel and his God. The Jews, however, heeded not their words, but stretched out their necks to be slaughtered for the sanctification of His Holy Name. Among them were the land's leading scholars as well as the men, women and children; the whole community. May the God of vengeance avenge them and return us to His land.

This tragedy was forewarned by King David (peace be unto him), in Psalm 32, where it is said: "For this (AL "ZOTH") let everyone that is godly pray unto Thee in a time when Thou mayest be found." (L'ETH

M'TZO) etc.,[8] so that no evil may come to pass. The letters of the words L'ETH M'TZO (in a time when Thou mayest be found), have the same numerical value as those of YAVAN V'KEDAR YACHDAV CHUBARU ("Greek" and Tartar joined together). The dog and the cat made an alliance to uproot the people of Israel, which is likened to a straying lamb. This occurred in the year (408) of the era of creation (ZOTH) omitting the first numeral. Psalm 69 also speaks of this tragic event.

There it is said: "Save me O God, for the waters are come in even unto the soul. I AM SUNK IN DEEP MIRE WHERE THERE IS NO STANDING. I am come into deep waters and the flood overwhelmed me . . . etc." [9] TAVATI B'YEVEN M'TZULAH (I am sunk in the deep mire), is of the same numerical value as CHMIEL VKEDAR B'YAVAN YACHDAV CHUBARU (CHMIEL and the Tartars joined together with the "Greeks"), the combined virus of a scorpion and a wasp.[10] "SHIBBOLETH" (the flood) is numerically equal to CHMIELECKI, HAYAVAN V'KEDAR (Chmielecki, the "Greeks" and the Tartars). SHETAFATNI SHETEF (anger and wrath overwhelmed me), for in the Polish language the name Chmielecki is associated with nobility, while the Russians referred to him as Chmiel.

Rabbi Jechiel Michael, chief of the Jewish community, and head of the academy of the holy congregation of Nemirow, whose soul departed in purity, for the glorification of His Name, referred to the name Chmiel, as representing the first letters of the phrase

AUTHOR'S INTRODUCTION 25

CHEVLE MASHIACH YAVI L'OLAM (he will usher in the pangs of the Messiah). And after him will come the feet of the messenger.

I named my book YEVEN M'TZULAH (THE DEEP MIRE), because the words of the Psalmist allude to these terrible events, and speak of the oppressors, the Tartars and the Ukrainians as well as of the arch-enemy, Chmiel, may his name be blotted out, may God send a curse upon him. This book may thus be a chronicle to serve future generations.

I dwelt at length on the causes which led to this great catastrophe, when the Ukrainians and the Tartars united to revolt against Poland, although the two had always been enemies. I recorded all the major and minor encounters, as well as the evil decrees and persecutions; also the days on which those cruelties occurred, so that everyone might be able to calculate the day on which his kin died, and observe the memorial properly. In addition, I have also described the customs and practices of Polish Jewry which followed the path of goodness and righteousness. All this I did with a deep reverence for God. I based these upon the six pillars which support the world.[11] I have written it in a lucid and intelligible style, and printed it on smooth and clear paper.

Therefore, buy ye this book at once. Do not spare your money, so that I may be enabled to publish the book "N'ta Shaashuim" (Plant of Delights), containing homilies on the Pentateuch which I have authored.[12] For this benevolence the Almighty God will keep you from all evil and distress, and will hasten the com-

this book is a means to the end for the author

Vernadsky's Bohdan: Hetman of Ukraine, Yale University

BOGDAN CHMIELNICKI

I

ABYSS OF DESPAIR

In the year (5)345 [1] of the era of creation King Sigismund of Sweden [2] ruled over the Kingdom of Poland, and in the year (5)352,[3] he married Anne, a woman of noble ancestry. She was the niece of Emperor Rudolph, and the daughter of Duke Carlos, who was the son of Emperor Ferdinand (of blessed memory). This I found at the end of the book "Tzemach David." [4]

The King was a kind and upright man. He loved justice and loved Israel. In his days the religion of the Pope [5] gained strength in the Kingdom of Poland. Formerly most of the dukes and the ruling nobility adhered to the Greek Orthodox faith, thus the followers of both faiths were treated with equal regard. King Sigismund, however, raised the status of the catholic dukes and princes above those of the Ukrainians, so that most of the latter abandoned their Greek-Orthodox faith and embraced Catholicism. And the masses that followed the Greek Orthodox Church became gradually impoverished. They were looked upon as lowly and inferior beings and became the slaves and the handmaids of the Polish people and of the Jews. Those among them who were trained warriors were conscripted by the King to serve in his army. This group numbered approximately thirty thousand fighting men, and they were called Cossacks. They were exempt from taxes to the King and the nobles. It was their specific task to guard the frontier which bordered the Province of [Little] Russia and the Kingdom of the Tartars, and to protect the country against attacks from the latter. For the Tartars had always been a "stone of stumbling and a rock of offense"[6] to the Kingdom of Poland. There always existed an abiding enmity between the Tartars and the Ukrainians, resulting in continuous warfare between them. The Cossacks therefore enjoyed special privileges like the nobility, and were exempt from taxes. The rest of the Ukrainians, however were a wretched and an enslaved lot, servants to the dukes and the nobles. "Their lives were made bitter by hard labor, in mortar and bricks, and in all manner of services in the house and in the field."[7] The nobles levied upon them heavy taxes, and some even resorted to cruelty and torture with the intent of persuading them to accept Catholicism. So wretched and lowly had they become that all classes of people, even the lowliest among them,[8] became their overlords.

II

THESE ARE THE RECORDS OF THE MASSACRES OF NALEVAIKO, (MAY HIS NAME BE BLOTTED OUT)

In the year (5)362,[1] according to the minor reckoning, the seventeenth year of the reign of King Sigismund, there arose a Ukrainian Priest, by the name of Nalevaiko [2] to avenge the cruel treatment accorded his people. He exhorted his people in the following words: "How long will ye keep silent at the cruelties perpetrated by the Polish people?" Gathering a large army of Ukrainians like the sand on the shore of the sea,[3] he staged a rebellion against the Kingdom of Poland, and conquered all of [Little] Russia up to the City of Cudnow.[4] When the King was apprised of this he sent two generals with all his army equipped with chariots and riders to wage war against Nalevaiko. The Polish army prevailed and they captured the enemy Nalevaiko alive. They brought him to the capital city of Warsaw to stand in judgment for the crime of rebelling against the King. Justice was meted out to him, while his people were still further enslaved. The Cossacks who supported him were punished by having the number of their privileged reduced to twenty thousand. The rest were compelled to pay taxes to the

King and the nobles. Thus the number of Cossacks which was originally thirty thousand was reduced by ten thousand. Henceforth, there were only twenty thousand Cossacks. And the land had rest.[5]

In the year 391, according to the minor reckoning, King Sigismund died,[6] after ruling over Poland for forty-six years. He was succeeded by his son Wladislaw in 392.[7] He ruled over the Kingdom of Poland sixteen years. He had married a woman of noble descent, the daughter of Kaiser Matthias, the sister of Kaiser Ferdinand, may his glory increase, who now sits on the throne in the city of Vienna, may the Lord preserve him. The queen died in the year 405,[8] according to the minor reckoning, and in the year 406 [9] he took another wife, the daughter of a French King and the sister of the present King of France.[10] Wladislaw was a kind and benevolent King, he loved justice and he loved Israel. Peace reigned in his days.

III

THIS IS A RECORD OF THE MASSACRES OF PAWLIUK, (MAY HIS NAME BE BLOTTED OUT)

In the seventh year of Wladislaw's reign, the year (5)339,[1] there arose a Cossack by the name of Pawliuk (may his name be blotted out), to avenge the wrong of his people and to rebel against the kingdom of Poland. And many rabble and riffraff gathered themselves unto him. They crossed the passages of the Black Sea called Behind the Threshold [2] and in Russian, Porogi. There the vast wilderness provided a convenient and an appropriate place to assemble this people. Each time the Ukrainians rebelled they fled to this place, for no man came there save the Cossacks. No sooner did the adventurer arrive there than Cossacks and Ukrainians in the hundreds and the thousands joined him. They then took counsel together to blot out the name of Israel (God forbid), in the manner characteristic of the ancient Greek Kings: "Proclaim publicly that you have no share in the God of Israel, or be killed." [3] They also partitioned the Kingdom of Poland among themselves, the above mentioned oppressor Pawliuk was to be their king in the capital city of Warsaw. But the Holy One, Blessed be He,

Who knows everyone's innermost thoughts, brought to naught their counsel and frustrated their designs, and brought retribution upon their heads. Nevertheless, upon their return from "behind the threshold" they destroyed (because of our many sins), many synagogues and killed approximately two hundred Jews. They also destroyed many churches, and killed many priests in the towns of Lachowce and Lubin and in their environs. The remainder fled to the Kingdom of Poland.

When King Wladislaw heard of this evil thing he delegated two generals, one Koniecpolski, and the other Potocki, along with a large army, headed by the great warrior Laszcz, to wage war against them. The aforementioned two generals were to attack from one side, while the warrior Laszcz who had with him six hundred troops, was to encircle them on the road. He was to attack by way of the forests. Thus Laszcz and his troops were on one side and the two generals on the other, while the Cossacks were in the center. The Polish people struck an effective blow, and the oppressor Pawliuk, who had aspired to be King in the capital city of Warsaw, was captured alive, together with his officers and counsellors. They were brought in iron chains before the King in Warsaw. There Pawliuk was "crowned." He was placed upon an iron chair. A special iron crown was placed on his head, and an iron wand in his hand. These, however, had been heated to a glow, beneath him was burning coal which he was forced to fan with his hand. Thus he burned

MASSACRES OF PAWLIUK

until he died. The other officers and advisers also received their due punishment.

When the King realized that the Cossacks were still rebellious, he meted out further punishment to them. Of the twenty thousand which prior to this rebellion had enjoyed special privileges, only six thousand were to receive them now, while the remainder was to be subject to taxes, like the rest of the wretched Ukrainians. To prevent another outbreak he placed over them captains of the Polish army.

All this, however, did not avail, "for there is no counsel and no understanding against the Lord." [4] "And the 'calf' came forth." [5]

IV

THE BRUTAL OPPRESSIONS OF CHMIEL

Now I shall begin to record the brutal oppressions caused by Chmiel (may his name be blotted out), in the lands of [Little] Russia, Lithuania and Poland, in the years '408, '409, '410, '411, '412,[1] according to the minor reckoning.

In the year '408,[2] according to the minor reckoning, the sixteenth year of the reign of King Wladislaw, there lived a Cossack in the town of Czehiryn,[3] and his name in Russian was Chmiel (may his name be blotted out), while in Polish he was called Chmielecki.[4] He was one of the officers of the hundreds of the Cossacks. He was very rich, possessing sheep and oxen, a very large multitude of cattle. He was wise to do evil; a man of sinister designs, and mighty in war. His place of residence was Czehiryn, which was under the rule of General Koniecpolski. The general was aware of this man and of his manner of speech. For, while he was soft spoken, he had "seven abominations in his heart;"[5] a man plotting iniquity, in the manner of all the Ukrainians, who at first appear to the Jews as friends, and speak to them pleasant and comforting words, beguiling them with soft and kind speech, while they lie with their tongues and are deceitful and untrustworthy.

BRUTAL OPPRESSIONS OF CHMIEL 35

The general was always apprehensive about this man and frequently spoke of him to his officers and counsellors. "I am fearful that out of this man will come misfortune to the kingdom of Poland." He often sought some pretext to kill him, but found none. For Chmiel was a very sly man and was aware of the thing. He was very cautious in warfare not to be suspected. When the general was about to die he instructed his son in all matters of warfare. The latter was at this time a "choronzhy," which is the Polish name for the King's banner bearer in time of war. Hence, he was called Choronzhy to this day. And thus spoke the general of Chmiel, may his name be blotted out, and he said: "You know this man Chmiel and his evil designs. Therefore, you must devise some pretext so that you will be able to remove him from the world."

One day, as the noble Choronzhy was comforted after the death of his father, he married a woman of noble descent, the sister of the nobleman Zamojsky. He lavished upon her much money, gold and silver, above his means (as this is the practice in the kingdom of Poland, both among Jews and Gentiles: When a marriage is arranged, one who possesses only one thousand gold pieces mortgages his property, and borrows additional money, so that he will be able to spend two thousand gold pieces). After the Choronzhy married this woman and spent all his money, he decided to take his wife on a journey beyond the Dnieper River, where the Cossacks lived, to be favored for her sake, and to receive many gifts from the people in honor of their marriage. Afterwards, he planned to have the

Cossacks join him in a sudden attack upon the Tartars, where he would find an abundance of booty. This was their customary practice from days immemorial. And thus he did. Assembling his whole army, chariots and riders, he and his wife set forth on the journey to his possessions beyond the Dnieper. When the nobleman and his wife arrived in Czehiryn they received an enthusiastic welcome and were favored with many gifts. In that city lived the Jew Zechariah Sobilenki who was its governor and administrator. He was the nobleman's tax farmer, as was the customary occupation of most Jews in the kingdom of [Little] Russia. For they ruled in every part of [Little] Russia, a condition which aroused the jealousy of the peasants, and which was the cause for the massacres.

And so, the nobleman nonchalantly asked the Jew: "You are the governor of the city, pray, tell me, who are among the wealthy of this city?" His intention was to find a pretext to make them give him much money. The Jew Zechariah replied: "These and these are the rich" and he included also the oppressor Chmiel, who was very rich and possessed sheep and cattle, a very large flock. When the nobleman heard this he recalled his father's exhortation regarding this treacherous man: "Whence came to him all this wealth?" he thought. "Surely it was robbed from my serfs, the people of my estate. Hence, it is all mine." The noble Choronzhy, therefore, appropriated one shed containing many hundred heads of cattle which amounted to about half of Chmiel's stock. The oppressor Chmiel, however, remained silent, so that the nobleman might

BRUTAL OPPRESSIONS OF CHMIEL

not become suspicious of him; also he would not dare to dictate to the nobleman what to do when the latter is regarded in his province as a King in his kingdom. But Chmiel subsequently proceeded to avenge himself on the nobleman. He informed the Tartars in writing as follows: "Be on guard, for our noble, the Choronzhy, together with his troops are about to attack you." The Tartars had been living tranquilly, unaware of the approaching attack. As soon as they heard of this they armed themselves with swords and with bows and went out to meet him. Realizing that his plans had been revealed and aware of his small number of troops as compared with those of the Tartars, the nobleman and his detachment retreated to his land in great shame. It was not known to him who was responsible for the evil that befell him.

It happened once that Chmiel and his friends, the Cossacks, sat together drinking wine at the inn of the Jew who was governor of the city. When they became intoxicated ("The secret goes out when the wine comes in") [6] Chmiel boasted to his friends: "I took vengeance upon the nobleman, who expropriated my flocks," and he proceeded to relate the whole story. At the same time, the Jew, seated at another table busying himself with his accounts, heard the story. Forthwith he informed the nobleman, and Chmiel was put in iron chains and placed in prison awaiting his death. But, there lived another Jew in that city whose name was Jacob Sobilenski, a close friend of Chmiel who counselled the latter to have his friends bail him out of prison, so that he would subsequently appear before the nobleman in the church and on bended knees plead for his life; he should state that the Jew had spoken a falsehood because of his enmity toward him; that his friends would testify to the truth of his words. This he did and he succeeded. The nobleman released him this time.

After a thorough investigation of the case, the nobleman came to the conclusion that the Jewish governor had spoken the truth, and he placed Chmiel into prison a second time. After this the nobleman and his wife left the city and proceeded to his principal city of Brody, in Little Poland. He had instructed the officer of the thousand of that city, to decapitate Chmiel and to deliver his head to him. Should he fail to do so, his own life would be taken. What did the oppressor Chmiel do? When his friends, the officers of the hundreds, came to visit him in prison, he said to them: "Why are you keeping silent? Know that the people of Poland are becoming more haughty each day. They enslave our people with hard work. Not only are the nobles our masters but even the lowliest of all nations rule over us. Today this is being done to me; tomorrow they will do it to you. Afterwards they will plow the field with our people as one plows with oxen. If you heed my counsel, you will approach the officer of the thousand and plead with him to release me in your custody, on the occasion of their festival of baptism, which is to be held tomorrow. At night you and I will escape, together with our belongings, by way of the ferry boats behind the Dnieper. There we will take counsel together as to what to do against the Polish

BRUTAL OPPRESSIONS OF CHMIEL

people." This they did. All the officers of the hundreds approached the officer of the thousand to have Chmiel removed from prison on their guarantee. At night all of them escaped behind the Dnieper to the wilderness. From there they dispatched letters to the settlements where the Ukrainians dwelt, urging them to join the rebels. The Ukrainians responded and some twenty thousand hoodlums joined them.

When the King and the nobles heard of this, they dismissed it with laughter, for they said: "They will fall into our hands again as they did in their previous attempts." Subsequently, two Polish generals, Potocki and Kalinowsky, together with a thousand trained troops, proceeded to the city of Korsun, where they prepared for battle. They encamped there to protect the river crossings, so that the enemy would not be able to cross to the other side. The beginning of the rebellion took place before Purim '408.[7] There, behind the Dnieper Falls, Chmiel conferred with his troops. He said to his people: "You know well that the Poles are mightier than we. They have the strength of lions and leopards; their faces are aflame. Who ever succeeded in a rebellion against them? Therefore, give heed, my people, to my counsel. Come, let us make peace with our enemies, the Tartars, and together we will make war upon them." And they replied to him: "We will do as you say." Chmiel, forthwith went to the King of the Tartars, together with all his troops, and made peace with him. They made a covenant together to wage war upon the Kingdom of Poland. They also made a pact between them to divide the booty. The

Tartars were to appropriate the spoil in men and the prey in cattle,[8] and the Cossacks were to take all the booty, such as gold, silver and clothes. (Midian and Moab made peace between themselves because of their hatred for Israel.) [9] And the two went together,[10] the Tartars and the Ukrainians. And they came by way of the desert, and by the way of forests, until they reached the Polish camp. One day preceding their arrival, they dispatched scouts to the Polish camp to discover the strength and the number of the Polish troops. The spies saw that the Poles were few in number; that they were encamped upon a hill, eating and drinking with abandon to the accompaniment of drums and dances. The scouts reported what they saw and said to them: "We should go up and possess it, for we are well able to overcome it. They are encamped securely and are unaware of us." [11] The scouts were ordered to dig pits and ditches and other obstacles on the hill and in the valley to prevent a possible escape for the enemy.

And it came to pass on Tuesday, the fourth day of the month of Sivan, '408,[12] that the Tartars and the Ukrainians attacked by way of the forests, from two sides. The Tartars attacked from one side and the Ukrainians from the other. When the Poles realized that evil had been determined against them; that they were also being attacked by the Tartars; that they were few in number compared with the Tartars and Ukrainians who numbered more than sixty thousand, they attempted to escape through the forest, the hill and the valley, but they fell into the ditches which were

BRUTAL OPPRESSIONS OF CHMIEL 41

dug for them. The Tartars and the Ukrainians had completely surrounded them. The Polish generals then implored them not to spill their blood on the earth but to take them captive. The Tartars granted their request and took captive the whole Polish army together with its two generals. They tortured them and placed iron chains upon the feet of the two generals, Potocki and Kalinowski.

When many of the Polish magnates became aware of Chmiel's success, and that his plans held out promise for future successes, they too, rebelled against the Kingdom of Poland, and made an alliance with Chmiel. They vowed to serve him as faithfully as they had served the King of Poland. Among them was the Choronzhy's captain who had been instructed to behead Chmiel. Chmiel appointed him captain over his own troops. Also the personal secretary and scribe to general Koniecpolski, who had since died, became the scribe of Chmiel. This scribe was a very clever man. He had knowledge of all the war strategy of the Kingdom of Poland. Thus he, together with other Polish nobles, now became the advisers of Chmiel. These became the foes of the Kingdom of Poland. "From the very forest itself comes the handle of the axe that fells it." [13] The same day on which the Polish army and its two generals were captured, also brought the evil tidings that King Wladislaw died, and the whole Kingdom of Poland became as sheep which have no shepherd. When the dukes and the nobles heard that their king had died, and that all the Polish nobles, the mighty warriors, and also the two generals were captured, they became disheartened. The hearts of the Jews melted like wax before the fire, for fear of the enemy. All the nobles, who governed the provinces beyond the Dnieper, and west of the Dnieper up to the City of Polannoe, fled for their lives. Had not God spared us one, all Jews would have perished as did the city of Sodom. In the midst of all the confusion Duke Wisniowiecki, of blessed memory, with his army were stationed beyond the Dnieper. He was a friend of Israel, and unsurpassed as a war hero. He and his people escaped by way of Lithuania, and with him escaped some five hundred Jewish citizens; each one with his wife and children. He carried them as on the wings of eagles until they were brought to their destination. If danger lurked behind them, he instructed them to proceed ahead; and if the danger was in front, he went before them as a shield and a buckler, and they followed him.

The Jews on this side of the Dnieper were informed of these dreadful events on the first day of the festival of Shabuoth.[14] All of them took flight on that day, unmindful of their gold and silver. They ran for their lives. All those in the province of Ostrog, as well as those over which Ostrog[15] had jurisdiction, such as Biala Cerkiew, Pawolocz, Cudnow, and Lubartow, and also the communities over which they had jurisdiction—all of them fled. Some ran to Polannoe, some to Zaslaw, some to Ostrog, the Capital, and Stary Konstantynow, for these were fortified cities. All the provinces of the city of Lwow, in the Kingdom of [Little] Russia, and the communities belonging to them such

BRUTAL OPPRESSIONS OF CHMIEL 43

as the environs of Nemirow, escaped to Nemirow, and those of the environs of Tulczyn fled to Tulczyn, and those of the environs of Bar, such as Winnice and Starygrod, and Krasne together with the communities adjacent to them, fled to the city of Bar. Whoever failed to escape or was unable to flee was killed. Many communities beyond the Dnieper, and close to the battlefield, such as Pereyaslaw, Baryszowka, Piratyn, and Boryspole, Lubin and Lachowce and their neighbors, who were unable to escape, perished for the sanctification of His Name. These persons died cruel and bitter deaths. Some were skinned alive and their flesh was thrown to the dogs; some had their hands and limbs chopped off, and their bodies thrown on the highway only to be trampled by wagons and crushed by horses; some had wounds inflicted upon them, and thrown on the street to die a slow death; they writhed in their blood until they breathed their last; others were buried alive. The enemy slaughtered infants in the laps of their mothers. They were sliced into pieces like fish. They slashed the bellies of pregnant women, removed their infants and tossed them in their faces. Some women had their bellies torn open and live cats placed in them. The bellies were then sewed up with the live cats remaining within. They chopped off the hands of the victims so that they would not be able to remove the cats from the bellies. The infants were hung on the breasts of their mothers. Some children were pierced with spears, roasted on the fire and then brought to their mothers to be eaten. Many times they used the bodies of Jewish children as improvised bridges upon which they later crossed. There was no cruel device of murder in the whole world that was not perpetrated by the enemies. All the four death penalties; stoning, burning, beheading and strangling [16] were meted out to the Jews. Many were taken by the Tartars into captivity. Women and virgins were ravished. They lay with the women in the presence of their husbands. They seized comely women as handmaids and housekeepers, some as wives and concubines. Similar atrocities were perpetrated in all the settlements through which they passed. Also against the Polish people, these cruelties were perpetrated, especially against the priests and bishops. Thus, westward of the Dnieper several thousand Jewish persons perished and several hundred were forced to change their faith. Scrolls of the Law were torn to pieces, and turned into boots and shoes for their feet; the straps of the phylacteries served as laces around their feet. The leather boxes of the phylacteries were cast into the streets. Other sacred books served to pave the streets. Some were used for kindling purposes, and others to stuff the barrels of their guns. The ears ring at the hearing of this.

When the Jews of Pogrobiszcze, of Zywotow, of Baziowka and Tetjew and their surroundings heard of what the Ukrainians perpetrated against our brethren beyond the Dnieper; that the Tartars and the Ukrainians surrounded them, the Tartars on one side of the city and the Ukrainians on the other, they said: "If we wait until the Ukrainians invade the city we will all either perish or we will be forced into baptism

(God forbid). It is preferable that we fall captive to the Tartars. For, we know that our brethren in Constantinople and in other Turkish communities, are very compassionate and they will ransom us." This they did. The four above mentioned communities, surrendered to the Tartars, men, women and children, some three thousand souls. Among them there was a cantor, Reb Hirsh of Zywotow. When the Tartars came into the city, he began to chant mournfully the Memorial prayer, El Maleh Rachamim (O God full of compassion) on behalf of our slaughtered brethren of the house of Israel. All the people burst forth with intense weeping. Apparently, their cries ascended on high, for the compassion of their captors was stirred. They consoled them with expressions of sympathy and said to them: "Do not despair, and do not deny yourselves food or drink. There are ritual slaughterers among you; let them kill an abundance of sheep and oxen for your need, and forthwith we will bring you to your brethren in Constantinople to be ransomed." The Tartars kept their promise. Our brethren in Constantinople, the Lord preserve them, redeemed them, together with other Polish captives, numbering approximately twenty thousand souls. They expended vast sums of money, all that was asked of them. They provided food and shelter for them to the present day; they favored them with many services without limit. The entire land of Turkey manifested such generosity, especially the people of the city of Salonica, may the Lord preserve them. They ransomed a large number of captives. The renowned city of Venice, the crown city of Rome, and the beloved and laudable city of Livorno, as well as other holy communities of Italy contributed many thousands and tens of thousands of gold pieces which were forwarded to greater Constantinople (the Lord shield her) for the ransoming of the captives. The Lord recompense these good people for the kindness shown to our brethren of the house of Israel, and keep them from evil until the coming of the Redeemer.

Following these events, the Tartars returned to their land with all their prize, and the oppressor Chmiel, together with his Cossack troops and many thousands of Tartars, who had remained with him, went to his city of Czehivyn. They approached the city with triumphant fanfare. All the people of the city came out to welcome him with timbrels and dancing and with great rejoicing. They blessed him and hailed him as prince and leader over them and their children after them. And they said to him: "You are a prince of God [17] and our liberator. You have redeemed us from the Polish nobles who oppressed us with hard labor."

And it came to pass when the oppressor Chmiel, reposed in his home, he addressed himself to his servants, ministers and advisers, and said to them: "Come let us take counsel together, so that we will not be regarded with shame and derision by our enemies, for we are abhorred by the inhabitants of the land of Poland, and when the Catholic kings will hear of the evil we have perpetrated they will make war upon us, and we are but few in number." And they replied to him: "This is the counsel we offer; that you send letters to the Polish nobles and dukes, words of peace and truth,[18] words of comfort and sympathy. Tell them that you regret all you have done; that all was imperative in order to save yourself. This you must do so that they will not mobilize troops against us speedily. Meanwhile, send messengers to the King of the Tartars to supply you with additional troops. Also, send letters to all Ukrainians in the Kingdom of Poland to be prepared for the appointed time to gather themselves together, and to stand for their life, to avenge themselves on their enemies, the nobles and the Jews." This he did. He sent secret messages to all the provinces, and to every place where groups of the Ukrainian people lived to be prepared for the appointed time, to gather themselves together and to stand for their lives,[19] to destroy, to slay, and to cause to perish all the Jews, and all the army of Poland that would assault them; their little ones and their women, and to take their spoil for a prey. When the thing became known to the Jews through their friendly Ukrainian neighbors, and also through their own spies who had been placed in all their settlements, they notified their lords, the nobles. Immediately messages were sent forth from community to community by means of horse riders, informing the Jews and the nobles of daily developments. In recognition of this the nobles befriended the Jews exceedingly and became united with them in one band, like one soul. For the Holy One blessed be He, sends the cure before the plague. Had it not been for this action there would have been no escape for the remnant of Israel

(God forbid). And in every province whithersoever the oppressor's command and his decree came [20] there was great rejoicing among the Ukrainians, and great mourning among the nobles and Jews, and fasting and weeping and a bitter cry, and repentance and prayer and charity. All this notwithstanding, His anger did not abate and the oppressor's hand yet remained outstretched. The Lord have compassion upon them.

Meanwhile Chmiel sent messages to the dukes and nobles, words of peace. He wrote to them words of comfort and sympathy. Everything that he had done had been inevitable in order to save those who were condemned to death. "If one comes to slay thee, forstall and slay him," [21] and "The persecuted are not accountable for their deeds." [22] He also advised the nobles to return to their homes, and he would return their estates to them. But the nobles paid no heed to his messages, for they understood that all this was falsehood and deceit; that he was merely seeking to ensnare them. They instinctively felt that all this was misrepresentation and deception; that it would be a "dark peace," indeed. For while he was offering them peace, he proceeded to put all of [Little] Russia under his rule and he received taxes from all the estates that formerly belonged to the nobles. They also recalled his deeds beyond the Dnieper against the Jews and the nobles; how he destroyed their churches and slew their priests. All this he did after capturing the Polish army. Consequently, they did not believe his words. They sent letters to the Archbishop, or as he was known in Italian, the Cardinal, whose seat was in Gniezno, and who was

BRUTAL OPPRESSIONS OF CHMIEL

regent because of the King's death so that Poland should not be without a government. "But for the fear of it man would swallow each other alive." [23] At this time the Cardinal of Gniezno was one Casimir, may His glory increase, who caused his enemies to fall under him. All the dukes and nobles notified him that they had unanimously agreed that he be appointed commander, so that the Kingdom of Poland will not be like sheep without a shepherd. Immediately Cardinal Casimir handed the ruler's wand, which is called in Polish Bulawa into the hands of Duke Wladislaw Dominick, may His glory increase, the Archduke of Zaslaw. This duke brought additional distress to Israel, and to the Kingdom of Poland. He was famed for his great wealth but was never experienced in warfare. For he was fearful and faint hearted, and only because of his tremendous wealth did the Cardinal appoint him as general. "When the shepherd is wroth with the sheep he blinds their leader." [24] This was the case in Poland (because of our many sins). The Cardinal also announced, under threat of punishment, throughout Poland, that all nobles should mobilize to wreak avengeance on their enemies. Unfortunately, they assembled very slowly, as was characteristic of the Kingdom of Poland. Whenever they engaged in war they always proceeded slowly and without dispatch. The contrary is the case with the Tartars and the Ukrainians. They proceed with haste, not with indolence.

V

THE MASSACRES OF THE HOLY COMMUNITY OF NEMIROW

The Oppressor Chmiel, may his name be blotted out, heard that many Jews had gathered in the holy community of Nemirow, and that they had a great deal of silver and gold with them. He knew that the holy community of Nemirow was distinguished for its great riches. It had been a great and important community replete with scholars and scribes, a city full of justice, the abode of righteousness, (but now they have been murdered).

Accordingly, Chmiel, sent a leader, an enemy of the Jews, and about six hundred swordsmen with him, to attack this noble community. In addition, he wrote to the city heads to help the band. The city leaders readily responded to aid them with all their might and main. This they did, not so much because of their love of the Cossacks but because of their hatred of the Jews.

And it came to pass on a Wednesday, the 20th of Sivan,[1] that Cossacks approached the city of Nemirow. When the Jews saw the troops from afar, their hearts trembled from fright, though they were not certain, as yet, whether they were Polish or Cossack. Nevertheless all the Jews went with their wives, and infants, with their silver and gold, into the fortress, and locked and barred the doors, prepared to fight them. What did those evil-doers, the Cossacks do? They devised flags like those of the Poles, for there is no other way to distinguish between the Polish and the Cossack forces except through their banners. The people of the city were fully aware of this trickery, and nevertheless called to the Jews in the fortress: "Open the gate. This is a Polish army which has come to save you from the hands of your enemies, should they come." The Jews who were standing guard on the wall, seeing that the flags were like those of Poland, believed that the people of the city spoke the truth. Immediately they opened the gate. No sooner had the gate been opened than the Cossacks entered with drawn swords, and the townspeople too, armed with swords, spears and scythes, and some only with clubs, and they killed the Jews in large numbers. Women and young girls were ravished,[2] but some of the women and maidens jumped into the moat surrounding the fortress in order that the uncircumcized should not defile them. They drowned in the waters. Many of them who were able to swim, jumped into water, believing they would escape the slaughter, but the Ukrainians swam after them with their swords and their scythes, and killed them in the water. Some of the enemy shot with their guns into the water, and killed them till the water became red with the blood of the slain.

The head of the rabbinical academy of Nemirow was also there. His name was, his excellency, our master and teacher, the rabbi; Rabbi Jechiel Michael, son of his excellency, our teacher, Rabbi Eliezer,[3] of blessed memory. He knew the whole of Rabbinic writings by heart and was proficient in all the worldly sciences. On the Sabbath before the catastrophe he preached and admonished the people that if the enemy should come (God forbid) they should not change their faith, but rather be martyred for the sanctification of His Name. This the holy people did. He also jumped into the water believing that he would save himself by swimming when a Ukrainian seized him and wanted to slay him, but the scholar implored him not to kill him, for which he would compensate him with a great deal of gold and silver. The Ukrainian consented and he led him to the house, where his silver and gold were hidden, and the Cossack released him. The Rabbi then left that place with his mother, and the two hid in a certain house all that night till the morning dawn.

On the morrow, the 22nd of Sivan, the Ukrainians searched the houses, suspecting that Jews might be hidden there. The Rabbi and his mother then fled to the cemetery. Thus, should they be killed they would receive burial. But it so happened that when they came near the cemetery, a Ukrainian shoemaker, one of the townspeople, pursued the Rabbi with club in hand and inflicted on him wounds. The Rabbi's mother pleaded with the Ukrainian to be killed instead of the son but the latter paid no attention and proceeded to kill first the Rabbi and then the mother, may God avenge their blood. Three days after the massacre the Rabbi's wife buried him, for in the town where the slaughter took

MASSACRES OF NEMIROW

place the majority of the women were spared, except for the old and feeble who were killed.

It happened there that a beautiful maiden, of a renowned and wealthy family, had been captured by a certain Cossack who forced her to be his wife. But, before they lived together she told him with cunning that she possessed a certain magic and that no weapon could harm her. She said to him: "If you do not believe me, just test me. Shoot at me with a gun, and you will see that I will not be harmed." The Cossack, her husband, in his simplicity, thought she was telling the truth. He shot at her with his gun and she fell and died for the sanctification of the Name, to avoid being defiled by him, may God avenge her blood.

Another event occurred when a beautiful girl, about to be married to a Cossack, insisted that their marriage take place in a church which stood across the bridge. He granted her request, and with timbrels and flutes, attired in festive garb, led her to the marriage. As soon as they came to the bridge she jumped into the water and was drowned for the sanctification of the Name. May God avenge her blood. These, and many similar events took place, far too numerous to be recorded. The number of the slain and drowned in the holy community of Nemirow was about six thousand. They perished by all sorts of terrible deaths, as has already been described. May God avenge their blood. Those of the holy community of Nemirow who escaped the sword fled to the holy community of Tulczyn, for there, outside the city, was a very strong fortress.

VI

THE MASSACRES OF THE HOLY COMMUNITY OF TULCZYN

And it came to pass after the evil doings in the holy community of Nemirow, that a band of about ten thousand men, scoundrels, and hooligans, assembled together under the leadership of the oppressor of the Jews, Krzywonos,[1] may his name and memory be blotted out. They proceeded from there to the holy community of Tulczyn, for there, in the fortress were assembled some six hundred Polish troops and with them were gathered some two thousand Jews. Among the latter were also trained soldiers and seasoned warriors. The Jews and the nobles made a covenant to help each other in the struggle against their common enemy, and took an oath not to betray one another. They reinforced the fort, and, armed with all kinds of weapons, the Jews and the nobles took their posts on the rampart. Each time the Ukrainians drew near the fortress, the defenders on the wall shot at them with arrows and bullets, inflicting heavy losses on them. They fled from the Jews, and the latter summoned courage and pursued them, killing hundreds of their men.

The Ukrainians assembled again, and together with the villagers and the inhabitants of the nearby communities, numbering in the thousands and tens of thousands, stormed the fortress. They employed iron battering rams to pierce the wall. With wild shouts and strange yelling, characteristic of the Cossacks, they made a sudden attack on the wall. When those stationed on the wall saw the multitude, their hearts trembled. Yet they continued to shoot from the wall and did not allow them to come near it. This time too, the Jews repulsed them.

After a lapse of several days the Ukrainians took counsel together and agreed to send a peace offer to the nobles in the fortress. They would conclude a truce on condition that the Jewish spoil be delivered to them as a ransom for their lives. This they did, and a message of peace was sent to the nobles in the fortress. The nobles immediately agreed to accept the offer. They sent for the Jews to disarm them one by one until all were disarmed. The Jews understood the trickery and wanted to lay hand upon the nobles first, and to rise against them, since they were the first to betray the covenant. But the president of the Rabbinical Academy of the holy community of Tulczyn, the scholar, our teacher and Master, Rabbi Aaron, cried aloud to the Jews: "Hearken, my brethren and my people. We are in exile among the nations. If you will lay a hand upon the nobles, and the Catholic kings will hear of it, they will wreak vengeance upon our brethren in exile (God forbid). Therefore, if our fate be decreed from Heaven, let us accept the judgment with rejoicing. We are not worthier than our brethren of the holy community of Nemirow. And may the Almighty be merciful unto us in the face of our enemies. Perchance, they will accept our possessions as a ransom for our lives."

And the Jews hearkened to him, and brought into the courtyard of the fortress all their valuables which they had salvaged. No sooner did the Ukrainians enter than the leader of the nobles, Duke Cwierczynski, said to them: "Behold, here is your prize which you requested." And they took all the booty of the Jews. The Ukrainian oppressors then ordered the above mentioned duke to imprison all the Jews, so that their lives would hang in doubt, for they would not know what their judgment might be; whether they would keep their promise or not. On the third day when they were in pain,[2] the Ukrainians came to the nobles and asked that all the Jews be delivered to them. Immediately the Jews were shoved out of the fortress, so that the nobles might escape injury. Brokenhearted and downcast, all the Jews walked out. The Ukrainians assembled them in an enclosed garden so that they would not escape. There they remained for a long time.

There were three other great scholars among them. His excellency, our teacher and master, Rabbi Eliezer; his excellency, our teacher and master, Rabbi Solomon, and his excellency, our Teacher, Rabbi Chaim. They exhorted the holy people to sanctify the Name and not to change their faith. All of them replied: "Hear O Israel, the Lord our God, the Lord is One. As there is but One in your hearts, so is there but One in our hearts."

After these things one of their intermediaries appeared, and planting a banner in the ground, he said to them in a loud voice. "Whoever wishes to change his faith and remain alive, let him sit under this banner." No one answered him. Thus he announced three times, and no one responded. Immediately the gate of the garden opened, and the infuriated mob rushed in and killed a large number of Jews. Approximately fifteen hundred souls perished by all sorts of terrible deaths. The three scholars, mentioned above, fell by the sword. May God avenge their blood. Then the Ukrainians took ten rabbis and placed them in prison, in irons, to await their ransom for ten thousand gold pieces. Among them was the scholar, our teacher and master, Rabbi Aaron, the son of the scholar, our teacher and master Rabbi Meir; the merciful God keep him and redeem him. The latter was the president of the Rabbinical Academy of the holy community of Lwow, and a very wealthy man, and the Ukrainians knew that he would ransom his son at any price.

After the slaughter of the Jews they proceeded to attack the fortress. And the nobles said to them: "Behold, you made an agreement with us, why do you repudiate your pledge?" And the Ukrainians replied: "As you did unto the Jews, breaking your promise to them, so shall we do unto you; measure for measure." When those stationed on the wall began to shoot, the Ukrainians cunningly set the fortress afire, killing all the nobles and countless others. They appropriated the spoil for a prey. The wife and the two daughters of the above mentioned Duke were raped in the presence of their father prior to his death.[3] He had been a very stout man. When he sat in a chair he was unable to rise. One of the scoundrels, a former slave, who served in his flour mill approached him, and, removing his hat in mockery and jest, said: "What does the master desire of his servant?" Then he recalled to him the mistreatment of his serfs, the beatings, and the enslavement and he said to him: "Stand up and I will sit in your chair and be your master." But the Duke was unable to rise. The slave then hurled him off the chair, and on the threshold of the house he brutally cut off his head with a saw. As they did so did God repay them, because they violated the pledge of the Jews. When the nobles heard of this, they were stricken with remorse and henceforth supported the Jews and did not deliver them into the hands of the reprobates. And even though the Ukrainians repeatedly promised the nobles immunity they no longer believed them. Were it not for this, there would have been no escape for the remnant of the Jews (God forbid).

After three days of carnage the Ukrainians announced among the slain: "He that is still alive may rise and need not fear, for the massacre is over." Some three hundred individuals who had sought escape by mixing with the corpses, arose. They were starved and thirsty. Some of them were wounded but not critically. With but the breath of life in their aching and weak bodies, fatigued, barefoot, and naked, they walked to the above mentioned city. The Ukrainian inhabitants of the city dealt kindly with them and sent them away.

After the scoundrels perpetrated the evil in the holy community of Tulczyn they returned home with a

MASSACRES OF TULCZYN

great deal of spoil of silver, gold, precious stones and diamonds, which they had taken from the nobles and Jews. In addition, they took into captivity many beautiful women and maidens, Jewish and Polish, and the ten Rabbis.

When the Dukes and the nobles heard of the evil deeds which the Ukrainians wrought in the cities of Nemirow and Tulczyn they became frightened and a feeling of vengeance, like the venom of a snake, possessed them. They agreed to mobilize all the Polish nobles to avenge their brethren. By order of the Cardinal, the general announced throughout the kingdom of Poland: "He that is an officer, and has his name registered among the King's troops shall enlist for war or send his servant in his place."

Duke Wiśniowiecki, of blessed memory, and his troops were at this time in Lithuania. When he heard what had happened to the Jews in Nemirow he was grief-stricken. For Nemirow was under his rule. Mobilizing his forces, he and his people, some three thousand men, proceeded to Nemirow to avenge the Jews. He vowed that he would not relent until he bathed in the blood of his enemies, the Ukrainians, who destroyed many other provinces, beyond the Dnieper, under his jurisdiction, and expelled the people from his domain. When he came close to Nemirow he sent several hundred troops into the city and they killed a large number of the local inhabitants. After this the remaining Ukrainians deceived the Duke by asking him to send several hundred of his troops to protect the city against the Cossacks and the Tartars. They promised to support him in his war against the enemies with all their might, and to serve him faithfully from that day on. They took an oath on this. The Duke was pleased with this offer and sent to them many nobles and six hundred of his best troops. The people of the city received them with great honor.

Several days later the inhabitants notified the Cossacks: "Make haste and come here at night. We will open the gates for you." This they did. All the nobles were killed while sleeping in their beds. The Cossacks were then persuaded, for a considerable sum of money, to remain in the city to protect it against additional attacks from the Polish nobles.

When the Duke was apprised of this treachery his heart trembled. He refrained from sending additional troops. Instead, he turned from there to avenge his people on the Cossacks in other places. He went to Machnowka, and killed there and in its environs a large number of Cossacks.

When Chmiel heard that Duke Wiśniowiecki was approaching his camp, and that he had inflicted a great blow on his people, small as his army was, only three thousand men, he delegated his general Krzywonos, may his name be blotted out, together with ten thousand of his best troops to engage him in battle. He instructed him to take the Duke alive, should he prevail. But God helped the Duke and saved him from their hands.

When the aforementioned Duke and his people heard that a large army of Cossacks was about to attack them, and that he was being surrounded on every side by the Ukrainians, he withdrew from the city in order not to be encircled, and proceeded to Berdyczow. There, resided Tyszkiewicz, the Voyevoda,[4] who had a thousand seasoned troops. The Duke and the Voyevoda joined forces and with four thousand troops marched close to Poland. They had written to the General, Duke Wladislaw Dominik to send them additional troops to help them, but the latter withheld the troops from coming to their aid. The General had been an enemy of Duke Wiśniowiecki because the people had once preferred the latter to be general, for he was beloved and renowned throughout the land as a mighty warrior. He therefore hoped that Duke Wiśniowiecki would fall into the hands of his enemies.

And the two marched together; the aforementioned Duke and the Voyevoda together with their troops moved up to one mile past the city of Polannoe. The Cossacks and the Tartars were close behind them. Additional troops from the Ukrainian people assembled; altogether, about twenty thousand men. The Ukrainians and the Tartars then besieged the city of Polannoe.

VII

THE MASSACRES OF THE HOLY COMMUNITY OF POLANNOE

And it came to pass on Tuesday, the first day of the month of Av,[1] that the Tartars and the Ukrainians besieged the city of Polannoe. They prepared the attack against this city in which were nobles and Jews. The sentries on the wall, however, shot at them and they were unable to come close to the city, for there were among the defenders some two thousand Polish nobles, seasoned warriors, and some twelve thousand Jews who were also mighty fighters. This city, in which the nobles and the Jews took refuge, was fortified strongly with a double wall, and a moat surrounded it. Hence, there was no need to guard it except from that side which was adjacent to two settlements inhabited by some Ukrainians. The nobles, therefore, placed their strongest serfs to guard the side which needed most protection against the enemy. "The protectors of the city, however, became the destroyers of the city,"[2] for among the serfs of the nobles who stood guard on the wall were also Ukrainians. They were known in the Polish language as Haiduki (mercenaries) and they turned traitors.

On Wednesday, the second day of Av, the enemy

captured the two settlements which were inhabited by Ukrainians. These agreed to lend their assistance in the attack against the fortified city of the nobles and the Jews. The attack lasted all that Wednesday. On Thursday, the enemy called to the serfs of the nobles who were standing guard on the wall: "Behold we are brothers. Why are you aiding the nobles to fight against us? Is it not to your advantage to serve us than to serve those who are not of our people?" Subsequently, the serfs rebelled and only pretended to fight against them but permitted the Ukrainians to place ladders on the wall. Thus on Thursday the fortified city was captured. At once thousands of Ukrainians with drawn swords entered the city and began to massacre the people. When the nobles and the Jews saw that there was evil determined against them, and that the city was captured, those nobles who were horseriders fled to one side but the unfortunate Jews guarding the city were not permitted to escape, and they were killed for the glorification of the Name. Some ten thousand souls perished by the most terrible deaths the world has ever witnessed. They stretched their necks to the slaughter. A single Ukrainian invading a dwelling which housed several hundred Jewish persons would kill all of them and would meet no resistance.

Among them was a wise and understanding and divinely inspired Kabbalist whose name was, Our Teacher and Master Rabbi Samson of the holy community of Ostropole.[3] An angel would appear to him every day to teach him the mysteries of the Torah. This mystic composed a commentary on the Zohar based upon the Kabbalah of the Ari,[4] of blessed memory, but it was never published. The angel had told him prior to the massacre, to indulge in sincere repentance so that the evil decree will not come to pass. He preached frequently in the synagogue and exhorted the people to repent so that the evil would not come to pass. Accordingly all the communities repented sincerely but it did not avail, for the evil decree had already been sealed.

When the enemies and the oppressors invaded the city, the above mentioned mystic and three hundred of the most prominent citizens, all dressed in shrouds, with prayer shawls over their heads, entered the synagogue and engaged in fervent prayer. When the enemies arrived they killed all of them upon the sacred ground of the synagogue, may God avenge their blood. Many hundreds who managed to survive were forced to change their faith and many hundreds were taken captive by the Tartars.

We were informed in the holy city of Zaslaw that the Tartars and the Ukrainians were besieging the holy community of Polannoe. For, a messenger would be sent daily to observe the developments there. On that Tuesday he was unable to reach the city because of the besieging enemy. On Wednesday the messenger returned to us with the evil tidings that the enemies were besieging the holy community of Polannoe. And Zaslaw was only six miles from Polannoe. On that Thursday, whoever was able to flee, fled. We abandoned our homes which were filled with all sorts of valuables such as merchandise and books, and other

MASSACRES OF POLANNOE

good things. We did not spare our possessions. We only thought of saving ourselves and our sons and daughters. Some escaped to the capital city of Ostrog which was the metropolis of [Little] Russia; a city famed for its scholars and scribes; one which combined scholarship and wealth. I, and my family and my father-in-law, his honor, the master, Rabbi Abraham of the holy community of Zaslaw, together with his family and relatives, fled to the holy community of Miedzyrzecze, two thousand els distance from Ostrog the capital. In the community of Ostrog and its adjacent community Miedzyrzecze lived more than ten thousand householders, each with his family. We wanted to tarry there for Sabbath Hazon [5] so that in the interim we would be informed of the situation in Polannoe, how things stood. When on Friday afternoon we arrived in Miedzyrzecze, a messenger came to us and related that the Duke of Zaslaw, General Dominik, is expected to arrive on that day, together with a large army, to aid Duke Wiśniowiecki in Polannoe against the besieging enemies. And thus it was. The Duke and one thousand warriors arrived. The great hero Laszcz and the rest of his army followed behind him. There was great rejoicing among us. After Sabbath Hazon we would return to our homes, we thought, for, we were only four miles distance from the holy community of Zaslaw. We also thought that he would be able to free our brethren, of the house of Israel, in the holy community of Polannoe, of their troubles.

On Sabbath eve we were stunned by the evil tidings

which reached us through the noble Wiszowaty, who was the governor of Polannoe. He and many other nobles had fled. He said: "Polannoe has been captured. All the nobles and the Jews therein were murdered and the enemy's onslaught is reaching Zaslaw. Duke Wiśniowiecki, together with his troops, fled to Konstantynow, and the Tartars and the Ukrainians are pursuing them. Some of them are marching toward Ostrog and Miedzyrzecze."

Then were the chiefs of Edom affrighted [6] and a great fear fell upon the Jews. No one was able to summon courage. Everyone's eyes were directed toward the general, Duke Dominik. What will he do?

And it came to pass in the middle of the night that the general Duke Dominik retreated through the very gate by which he arrived from Poland, for he feared to go through the main road to Konstantynow by way of Zaslaw because a large army of Tartars and Ukrainians were there while his men were few in number. He, therefore, followed a circuitous route and went to Krzemieniec, a distance of nine miles, by way of the woods. There he waited to be reinforced by additional Polish troops, in order to go to the city of Konstantynow. The mass of people, however, were under the impression that the general escaped to the Kingdom of Poland. They all said: "If a flame among the cedars fall, what avails the lichen on the wall?" [7] in other words, if the general flees, what is left for us to do? The heads of the community of Ostrog announced that no Jew should dare to remain in that community, nor for that matter, in the community of Miedzyrzecze, for the enemy is only two miles distant from us. We cannot put any trust in the inhabitants of the city who are Ukrainians, that they themselves would not harm us. All the people fled in accordance with the announcement. Whoever had a horse and cart traveled in it. Those who did not possess a horse and cart, even though they had sufficient money to buy them, would not wait, but took wife and children by the hand and fled on foot, casting away all belongings. Also, he who possessed a horse and wagon but was burdened with a heavy load of articles, books or other valuables, unloaded them from the wagon at the inn and handed them to the innkeeper in order to be able to travel lightly.

On that Sabbath Hazon three rows of horses and carts, moved along one next to the other in width, and for a stretch of seven miles, the entire distance between Ostrog and the holy Community of Dubno in length, the road was cluttered up with horses and carts, one behind the other and innumerable pedestrians. Within two hours on that Sabbath Hazon, three horseriders, one Jew whose name was Moses Tzoref of Ostrog, together with two nobles, ran after us. They said to us: "Why are you marching so slowly? Behold, the enemy is close behind us. They are now in Miedzyrzecze. We escaped with difficulty." Immediately there was such confusion and panic among our brethren of the house of Israel that it is indescribable. Everyone threw from his cart silver and gold, vessels, books, pillows and bed covers in order to be able to escape more quickly, to save the lives of his family. The field was cluttered with gold, silver and clothes, and no Jew paused to take them. This time the admonishing words of the Prophet came true: "They shall cast their silver in the streets." [8] Some cast away everything; horse and cart and all that was in it, and with only wife and children fled for their lives into the woods. Many women and men who had led their children by the hands, released them when this panic seized them, and ran for their lives into the woods and into the pits. This time the verse of Leviticus came true "And ye shall flee when none pursueth you," [9] for it was all a falsehood; the enemies, the Tartars, did not pursue us. The fear, however, was so great upon all of us that Sabbath Hazon that everyone thought the Ukrainians were pursuing him.

On the Sunday following Sabbath Hazon the truth became known to us. The general had not fled to Poland, but only journeyed to the city of Krzemieniec. Then the anxiety was relieved, and from that day on everyone slackened his pace. We walked from place to place through cities and villages, sleeping in the streets. And even then we found no rest for our weary souls. We were robbed and crushed, despised and hated. The admonishing verses of the Scripture: "And among these nations shalt thou have no repose, and there shall be no rest for the sole of thy feet," [10] etc . . ." and thy life shall hang in doubt before thee; and thou shalt fear night and day and shalt have no assurance of thy life," for every night that we spent in a Ukrainian inn we feared that the innkeeper would kill us in the night, because they were all rebels. When we arose in the morning alive we recited the prayer, "Blessed art Thou who quickenest the dead."

VIII

THE MASSACRE IN THE HOLY COMMUNITY OF OSTROG AND IN THE HOLY COMMUNITY OF ZASLAW

After the enemies captured the holy community of Polannoe, and did what they would unto it, they proceeded to the holy community of Zaslaw. They robbed the whole community, and killed some two hundred persons, who had been unable to escape because of sickness. Some had placed their trust in their Ukrainian friends that they would save them, and therefore, hid in the forests until the fury would pass. There they lingered for a long time, and almost expired of hunger and thirst. They chose death to life and said: "Come let us go to the city, for we prefer to be victims of the sword than of starvation." When they arrived in the city they were seized by their "friends," the Ukrainians, to be killed. They implored them to be killed on the cemetery so they would be buried there. They were granted the request and were led to the cemetery. The Jews entered the chapel on the cemetery and were killed there. Afterwards they set fire to the house. The Jews were then condemned to two kinds of death; beheading and burning. The Catholic priests of the city of Zaslaw were skinned alive, while the dukes who had been interred for a long time, were removed from their graves and tossed aside. "As a carcass trodden underfoot."[1] The gold and silver mausoleums were desecrated. The Catholic monasteries as well as our synagogues were destroyed and turned into stables for horses. This they also did in the holy community of Ostrog, the capital, where they killed the six hundred persons who had remained there.

IX

THE MASSACRE IN THE HOLY COMMUNITY OF KONSTANTYNOW

From there they turned, with all the troops, toward the holy community of Konstantynow. Duke Wiśniowiecki went out to meet them and inflicted upon them a heavy loss; and subsequently returned to Konstantynow. As they pressed closer to the city the Duke, fearful that the Ukrainian inhabitants of the city would rebel against him, since the enemies outside were also composed of Ukrainians, retreated from there. With him departed all of the glory from that city. Duke Wiśniowiecki and his troops, and those Jews who possessed horse and cart followed him. Those who did not provide for themselves horse and cart but placed their trust in Wiśniowiecki and his troops who had been in this city, remained there. When the Duke was only about one mile away from the city, the enemies entered it. It was Tuesday, the ninth day of Av.[1] Some three thousand Jewish persons were slaughtered, and their spoil was taken for a prey. Among those killed was the scholar, our teacher and master, Rabbi Asher who was head of the Rabbinnical court, and president of the Rabbinnical Academy of the holy community of Polannoe and also many other scholars whose names are not known to me.

MASSACRES OF KONSTANTYNOW

After the looting of the city of Konstantynow, Duke Wiśniowiecki sent a message to them: How long will they continue to destroy cities and kill innocent people. If they are prepared for war and have a large army, let them wage war on the battlefields. They selected for themselves the field near Lipowice, on the river,[2] five miles from the holy community of Konstantynow. And they prepared a battleground, camp opposite camp; the Cossacks and Tartars on one side of the river, and Duke Wiśniowiecki and his troops on the other side. Additional troops were added on both sides, including Chmiel together with all his Cossack troops and other Ukrainians, numbering approximately five hundred thousand men. Also General Duke Dominik, together with his Polish army, chariots and riders, numbering approximately thirty-thousand soldiers. Additional troops were further added to both sides. For about two months they stood opposite each other. About six hundred thousand Ukrainians headed by Chmiel and Krzywonos, may their names be blotted out, and about eighty thousand Polish troops, headed by Duke Dominik and Duke Wiśniowiecki. They possessed one hundred and fifty thousand vehicles loaded with food, drink, silver, gold vessels, and garments and an unlimited quantity of the royal treasures. The six hundred thousand Ukrainians were no match even for twenty thousand Polish troops, for the Ukrainians were village and city folk, who were armed with clubs and scythes and inexperienced in warfare. Their type of warfare consisted of loud and bitter shouting; everyone shouted to frighten the people. All their wars were fought with great cunning, but they did not possess trained warriors, except for a portion of the Cossacks, and a portion of the Tartars, numbering approximately twenty thousand. While the Polish army consisted of outstanding nobles and trained warriors.

On Sunday, the fourth day of Tishre, 409,[3] they battled against each other. The Polish army prevailed and Duke Wiśniowiecki inflicted a great blow on them all that Sunday. On that Monday he even grew stronger and killed thousands and tens of thousands of the Ukrainian troops. Had the nobles permitted to strike also on Tuesday, none of the enemies of Israel would have remained. They would have been forced to surrender their leaders to their former Polish masters, make peace with them, and serve them as in days of yore.

When Chmiel became aware of this, he devised a scheme. He sent letters to General Dominik, asking for a short respite on Tuesday, and on Wednesday the battle would be resumed. It was his intention to delay them until Thursday, because two Tartar generals were arriving to aid him. The name of one was Bey and the name of the other was Tuhay Bey. These had with them one hundred thousand veteran Tartar troops and they were only one day's journey from them. Duke Dominik granted his request to rest on Tuesday. And Duke Dominik and Voyevoda Tyszkievicz spoke to Duke Wiśniowiecki: "How long will you continue to bring destruction to the Ukrainians, who are our slaves. Who will plow our fields for us,

MASSACRES OF KONSTANTYNOW

and who will do other and sundry work in the houses and in the field? If we slay them we will no longer have any slaves. Over whom will we then be the masters?" And the Polish troops had compassion upon the Ukrainians and refrained from attacking them all day Tuesday. But the enemy showed no mercy to the Poles when they fell into their hands.

On that Tuesday, toward evening, one hundred thousand Tartar warriors arrived into the Ukrainian camp. And there was exultation in the camp of the Ukrainians and the Tartars. With timbrels and flutes and trumpets they created such a clatter of noise that they made the earth quake. The Polish people however, knew not the cause for their rejoicing. They captured a Ukrainian soldier and they brought him to the Dukes for questioning and he said to them: "One hundred thousand Tartar soldiers have come to our aid, and their faces are aflame, who can withstand them?" Another version relates that Chmiel sent messages to general Duke Dominik as follows: "Peace be unto you, our Lord, the archduke Wladislaw Dominik, general of the Polish army. I and my people are grateful to you for the favor you granted us and the compassion you showed me and my people, to give us respite on Tuesday. Because of this I give you warning and benevolent counsel, that you and all your people flee this night. For there came to me a multitude of Tartars as the sand of the sea, and it is impossible to stand up against them and against my people; let not the Kingdom of Poland fall into the hands of the Tartars. Because you have shown compassion to us we are reciprocating your favor. We shall not destroy any of the cities under your rule as we destroyed the other cities of the Polish nobles."

When the dukes and nobles heard this they became terrified, and in the middle of the night all the dukes and nobles fled from camp.

When at dawn on Wednesday the Polish troops observed that all the leading dukes and nobles fled from the camp they, too, fled, all who were able to flee. They left behind all the wagons and carts filled with supplies in charge of the officers of supplies. And they hastened and fled, all of them. They abandoned their tents, their horses and asses, scattering on the road silver and gold and clothes, to facilitate their escape.

When the Tartars and the Ukrainians came into the Polish camp and observed that no one was there, they did not believe that the Poles had fled. They thought: "Surely they have tricked us so as to ambush us in the field and to attack us suddenly from there." And they sent scouts to investigate and they saw, and behold, the road is cluttered up with clothes and arms which they cast away in their haste. The Tartars then pursued them. Thus the Ukrainians and the Tartars spread out all over the Kingdom of Poland, [Little] Russia and Lithuania, and in all the places of their habitations. When the news reached the Ukrainians they immediately rebelled against their masters and killed the nobles and the Jews that were to be found, by all manner of terrible deaths. This was a time of distress for the Jews, the like of which has not yet taken place. When the Jews heard of this they escaped to more fortified places, to the cities of Bar, Kamieniec-Podolski, Brody, the capital Lwow, to Buczacz, Jazlowice, Zolkiew, to Narol, Przemysl, Belz, the monastery in Sokal, and to Zamość, some fled to Wallachia and many fled to the cities beyond the Vistula.

X

THE MASSACRE OF THE KINGDOM OF LITHUANIA

The people of Lithuania [1] fled to Wilno and to Great Grodno, where the enemies did not appear. Many communities, however, where thousands of Jews had taken refuge, were destroyed and the Jews therein were killed. Thus, in the city of Homel countless thousands were martyred for the glorification of the Name. From there the enemies proceeded to Starodub where they caused a great slaughter among the Jews. Similar slaughters were perpetrated in Czernigow, in Brahin, and in Wlodawa, where many Jews had assembled. Approximately ten thousand persons perished there by all sorts of terrible deaths. In the remaining large Lithuanian communities Jews were killed in thousands and tens of thousands. May the Lord avenge their blood.

Of the people in the cities of Sluck, Pinsk, Brest-Litovsk, some escaped to greater Poland, and others by waterway, to Danzig, on the river Vistula. The hapless ones who remained in Brest-Litovsk, and in Pinsk were martyred in the hundreds, for the glorification of His Name. The enemies pursued many hundreds of wagons of fleeing Jews on the open field near Pinsk overtaking them in the narrow paths, and killing large numbers of them.

The Polish troops, however, avenged themselves on the Ukrainians of Pinsk. When the general, Duke Radziwil, in charge of the Kingdom of Lithuania, heard that the people of Pinsk rebelled and permitted the scoundrels to enter the city, he and several thousand Polish troops besieged the city and set fire to it on its four sides. The scoundrels within the city tried to escape in boats and all of them were drowned. Some were burned and killed. Thus the Jews were avenged.

The people of the city of Sluck were also avenged. The inhabitants of the city notified the scoundrels to hasten to come, assuring them that many Jews and nobles were hiding there and they would deliver them to the Ukrainians. But there were no Jews in Sluck; they had already fled. They did not trust the local people to fight the foe. When the scoundrels approached the city they were met with cannon fire from the wall and from the gate. They suffered heavy losses. As they fled, the local people pursued them, and they smote them to utter destruction.[2]

XI

THE MASSACRES OF THE HOLY COMMUNITY OF BAR

When the Polish troops fled from the camp, the Tartars and the Ukrainians looted the whole camp, taking an abundance of silver and gold, carts and the very best horses. Then Chmiel, together with his army and the Tartars, prepared to conquer the fortified cities in the Kingdom of Poland. He sent some of his forces to capture the city of Bar, because in that fortified city was a large settlement of Jews and nobles. When the enemies came close to the city, the gunners on the wall shot at them and they were unable to storm the wall. And they laid siege to the city for many days.

What did the local people, the Ukrainians, do? They dug a tunnel under the city and allowed the scoundrels to enter the city at night, and the enemies began to massacre the people. The Jews and nobles took refuge in the mighty fortress and they fortified it strongly. There were no Ukrainians among them. And the enemies laid siege to the fortress several days, and they built against it mounds and bucklers,[1] and they shot at them with big cannons, which they call in German, Roeder Biksen, until they subdued the fortress and killed all the Jews and the nobles therein, inflicting upon them the most violent deaths in the world, and they took the booty for prey. The number of the slain in the city of Bar was approximately two thousand Jewish persons.

And the oppressor, Chmiel, together with all his army, marched on the city of Konstantynow, and from there to Zaslaw and from there to the capital city of Ostrog—these communities had already been destroyed by the Ukrainians—and from there to Great Dubno. There, too, was a fortress which had not its equal in all the Kingdom of Poland, and it was under the rule of General Duke Dominik. When the Duke and the nobles had fled from the battle field, several hundred Jews who had hoped to take refuge in the fortress, remained there. As the scoundrels approached the city of Dubno, a general and eighty of the Duke's warriors entered the fortress and locked it with bolts and bars. They fortified the stronghold and did not permit a single Jew to enter. Thus all of the Jews were slain in front of the fortress, some eleven hundred Jewish persons. When Chmiel arrived in the city of Dubno, he was amazed at the strength of the fortress, and said that it would have been impossible to capture it, and the nobles were fools to have fled from it. In that fortress were stored great treasures of the Jews and nobles but he refrained from besieging it because of its strength.

From there he proceeded to the city of Brody which was under the rule of General Choronzhy,[2] who had been the enemy of Chmiel, and who had sought to kill him. Chmiel destroyed all the provinces under the

Choronzhy's rule, especially the city of Brody, his metropolis, which he devastated and set on fire. All the Jews and the nobles fled into the fortress, for it was formidable, having a double wall to protect it, and it was surrounded by a moat. Several thousand Jews and nobles took refuge in it. The enemy besieged the fortress many days but could not get to the wall, for the gunners shot at them with cannons, and killed large numbers of them. And the enemies were unable to capture them. Nevertheless, there was great terror among the defenders because of the plague which broke out within. "Without shall the sword bereave, and in the chambers, terror." [3] Approximately one thousand Jewish persons died of the plague. Plagues of great proportions broke out in all the other fortresses that were besieged by the enemies.

XII

THE MASSACRES IN THE CAPITAL CITY OF LWOW

And it came to pass after these things [1] that Chmiel, may his name be blotted out, and his army, proceeded to besiege the holy community of Lwow, one of the four largest communities in the Kingdom of Poland.[2] It was a godly community, renowned for its sages and scribes. When the enemies arrived they encamped in the valley facing the tall fort which was outside the city of Lwow. A burst of fire from the fort killed thousands of Ukrainians and Tartars. Because of the lack of water, however, the Poles were compelled to leave the fort and go to the city of Lwow. The inhabitants then set fire to all the houses which surrounded the wall so that the enemies would not be able to hide in them. Nevertheless, the enemies succeeded in capturing the fort, and afterwards they encircled the city. The people were fearful of leaving their houses because of the shell fire which continued to come from the fort. As a result of this, famine and plague spread in the city. "Without shall the sword bereave and in the chambers, terror." Some ten thousand souls perished of starvation and disease.

After a long siege by the enemies the city could still not be overpowered. Then they stopped up the reservoirs outside the city which supplied the people with drinking water, and the people had no water to drink. And all the people said: "Wherefore shall we die of hunger and thirst? Let us inform the enemies that we will give them all our possessions as a ransom for our lives." And the people of the city sent messages to Chmiel to offer a compromise; they would give him all their silver and gold as a ransom for their lives.

And the offer found favor in his eyes and he said to his followers: "What profit is it that we slay them? Let us take their money in ransom for their lives." And he sent his captain Glowacki, a former Polish officer who had rebelled against the Kingdom of Poland and vowed allegiance to him, together with several Cossack officers, into the city to discuss the terms of the compromise. The city also sent forth several reputable nobles together with Reb Simeon Shtadlan [8] of Lwow, to visit Chmiel, and to discuss the matter with him. They agreed to the following compromise: two hundred fifty thousand gold pieces should be raised from among the Jews and the nobles in the entire city as a ransom for their lives. But this exorbitant sum could not be raised from among them, so they surrendered their silver and gold and other valuables, at a rate of exchange below the current value. They weighed the gold and the silver with weights as heavy as lead and half was given away for a mere pittance. And the Cossacks drained the city as one drains a fishpond. Were it not for God's compassion upon his people Israel, who were there in the thousands and in the tens of thousands, all of them renowned sages who did great

Upper—Synagogue in Zolkiew
Lower—Synagogue in Szaragrod

penance until their cry reached on High, and the Lord, blessed be He, inclined the heart of the scoundrels to compromise with them; had they been under siege but one more week, all the people of the city would have died of hunger and thirst.

From there they journeyed and besieged the city of Zolkiew. They attempted to approach the wall in order to place ladders on it, but the defenders poured scalding water on them forcing them to retreat. The gunners then shot at them with cannon and killed many of them. And the scoundrels took counsel together and said: "Behold, it is better for us to inform the people that we want to negotiate a compromise similar to the one we negotiated in Lwow." And they sent a message to the people of the city, and they said to them: "You are not stronger than the defenders of Lwow who were unable to stand up against us, and were forced to make a compromise. Consequently, if you will compromise with us it will be well. If not, all of us will besiege you and we shall execute great judgments, and inflict terrible deaths on you, as we have done in other places." And the thing found favor in the eyes of the people of the city (that the scoundrels were willing to compromise) and they sent a priest, a nobleman and a Jew who hailed from Czernigow, in [Little] Russia, to negotiate the compromise with them. And they agreed that the people of the city should pay twenty thousand gold pieces, six thousand to the aforementioned Captain Glowacki. They departed from there, leaving several thousand Cossacks to guard the city so that other Cossacks might not attack it again. They followed the same procedure with all the fortresses in the kingdoms of Little Poland, Russia, Podolia and Lithuania, bringing upon the people distress and suffering.

In the strong and fortified city of Kamieniec-Podolski, and in the cities of Jazlowice, Buczacz, Komarno, Belz and in Sokal in the Monastery, the nobles and the Jews defended themselves and fired upon the enemies with the big cannons, inflicting heavy losses upon them so that the hooligans were unable to capture even one of the forts. They retreated from them in embarrassment, and did not even offer a settlement for money, nor were they given a token compensation. But disease and starvation in those places brought death to many thousands and tens of thousands of Jews.

Przemysl, a city famed for its scholars and scribes, was also besieged, and the city was almost captured, but the Lord in heaven had mercy on them, and a general by the name of Korniakt, together with six hundred troops, came to their aid and with ingenuity rescued the city. However, all the cities and villages up to the River San were destroyed.

XIII

THE MASSACRES OF THE COMMUNITY OF NAROL

From there they journeyed to the holy community of Narol and laid siege to the city. Tens of thousands of Jews, and thousands of nobles had assembled there, and there was not among them even one of the Ukrainian people. Three large settlements, one next to the other were there. The Jews wanted to flee from there but the city official did not permit them. He said to them: "Let us stand up against them and engage them in battle as did the other fortified places." When the enemies besieged the city, they offered to compromise with them. The Jews were willing to do so, but the city official rejected the proposal and they fought against them three days, inflicting a heavy loss on the enemies. Then, the arch-enemy Chmiel sent a large reinforcement of troops, as many as the sand of the sea, and they captured the city on the 17th day of Heshvan, 409,[1] and they slew first, the city official, Laszcz, and skinned him alive. They subjected him to all sorts of terrible tortures. Then they slew among the Jews more than twelve thousand persons by all sorts of terrible deaths, as mentioned above. Many were drowned in the water and several hundred locked themselves in the synagogue, but the enemies smashed through the doors, and killed all the Jews therein, and later set fire to the synagogue and burned it, together with all the slain. There was no massacre so horrible in the whole Kingdom of Poland as in the city of Narol. Many were taken by the Tartars into captivity. They set fire to the three settlements, and they destroyed them as the city of Sodom was destroyed.

A woman who remained alive, related to me that several hundred women, and children, and a few men survived the carnage. These had no food for five days and they ate human flesh. They cut off organs from the slain and roasted them on fire and ate them. Many thousands of the slain were eaten by dogs and swine. The survivors sent some men to the city of Przemysl, and provided them with several hundred gold pieces to buy linen for shrouds. The victims were thus brought to burial. May the Lord recompense them for their kind deeds.

XIV

THE MASSACRES OF THE HOLY COMMUNITY OF ZAMOSC

From there the oppressor Chmiel, together with all of his army of Tartars and Ukrainians, a great multitude, like the sand of the sea, journeyed onward and laid siege to the city of Zamość, a city with which none can be compared in strength. It possessed a double wall and a moat surrounded it. As soon as the enemies arrived there, the town folk burned all the houses near the wall so that the enemies would not be able to hide in them. They did not permit the enemy to come within one half mile of the city. Thus they held out for many days.

Meanwhile the enemy dispersed throughout the surrounding communities and caused horrible slaughters, in Tomaszow, in Szczebrzeszyn, in Turbin, in Hrubieszow, in Tarnigrod, in Bilgoraj, in Gora, in Krasznyk. In all of these cities they massacred thousands and tens of thousands of Jews. Also in the Province of Wolhynia; in Wlodzimierz-Wolynski in Lubomla, in Luck, and in Krzemieniec, and their environs they caused horrible slaughters, killing thousands of Jews. In the city of Krzemieniec one hoodlum obtained a slaughtering knife, and slaughtered several hundred

Jewish children, and asked his comrade, in mockery, whether they were "kosher" or "trefah." He replied: "They are trefah." He then threw them to the dogs. Afterwards he took one of the slain children and slashed its throat open and asked: "Is this kosher?" And the comrade replied: "Yes, it is kosher." He inspected the entrails, as one does with goats and sheep,[1] and he then carried it on a spear through the streets of the city and called: "Who wishes to buy goats and sheep?" The Lord avenge their blood.

Also in the narrow paths near Biechow, the scoundrels overtook several hundred carts of Jews and they killed all of them. Similar slaughters took place in many other communities, the fury of which cannot be recorded. Thus they devastated more than seven hundred communities, all the cities and settlements up to the Vistula River. Though they besieged the city of Zamość many days they were unable to conquer it, for a German general by the name of Weiher, together with six thousand trained German troops, defended the city. They released cannon fire from the wall and killed many of the enemy. Yet thousands of Jews died of starvation and of the plague which broke out in the city.

And it came to pass when they had been there a long time,[2] that the enemy contrived a scheme. By the use of witchcraft they let a viper soar in the sky, and they took unto themselves as a sign: "If the viper will turn his face toward the city, we will subdue it before us, and if he will turn his face toward us we will flee before them. And it came to pass at midnight, when they saw the viper ascending skyward, and he remained suspended for about a half hour with his face toward the city. After that he turned toward the camp of the Cossacks and the Tartars. They realized that this was an evil omen for them and that evil was before their faces. They forthwith dispatched a message to the inhabitants of the city and said to them: "Is it not better for you to compromise with us, as did the capital city of Lwow than to die of starvation?" When the people of the city heard this they readily agreed and compromised with them to pay twenty thousand gold pieces. After this the Tartars and the Ukrainians drew near the wall and brought with them many prisoners to be ransomed. The Jews of the city ransomed several hundred prisoners. May the Lord recompense them for their kindness.

The oppressor, Chmiel, together with his Ukrainian and Tartar forces journeyed onward, and turned toward the Metropolis of Lublin, one of the four great communities in the Kingdom of Poland; a city unequaled in scholarship, worldly affairs, and loving kindness. The townspeople had fled from this city to take refuge beyond the Vistula River, leaving behind them several hundred citizens of the poorer class. They supplied them with sufficient money to provide for the indigent of the city, especially the refugees who came from other places. In the meantime all the nobles and the dukes of the Kingdom of Poland had gathered in Cracow, Poland's metropolis, to elect a king for themselves, so that the Kingdom will not be like sheep without a shepherd. The nobles and dukes deliberated but could not reach an agreement among them as to who shall rule over them. Some preferred Casimir, may his glory increase, the Cardinal of Gniezno. Others preferred his brother, Carlos, and still others preferred the Lord of Siebenbürgen in the Kingdom of Hungary, whose name was Rakoczy.

When the oppressor Chmiel heard about this he sent emissaries to the dukes and nobles in Cracow, saying: "If they will elect Casimir, the Cardinal of Gniezno, as king he will withdraw and will no longer wage war against them."

When the dukes and the nobles heard of this, it found favor in their eyes and they elected Casimir, the second son of King Sigismund, as king.

And it came to pass in the year 5409, in the month of Cheshvan, that our Lord, King Casimir, may his glory increase, was crowned.[3] May his Kingdom grow and may he cause his enemies to fall under him and behold seed, and be blessed with length of days. For he is a just King, a God-fearing man and a friend of Israel. He took unto himself the wife of his deceased brother, Wladislaw, for a wife.

After the King sat securely on the throne of his Kingdom, he dispatched letters to the oppressor, Chmiel, to return to his home, together with his army; that all his grievances against the Kingdom of Poland would be settled by mutual agreement.

The oppressor Chmiel, together with his forces, were on the way to capture the city of Lublin. When they were only four miles away from the city, the King's letter advising him to return home, reached him. He welcomed the King's letter with joy and immediately returned home. All that winter the land rested from war. Surely the merit of the people of Lublin, who dealt kindly with their brethren of the House of Israel who had escaped the sword; with the living as well as with the dead, was great. This kindness stood in their good stead, and saved them from the enemy's sword. However, throughout the period of the siege by the enemies, the city of Lublin was shut and closed. No one went out or came in. And there was a great plague in the city, and more than ten thousand Jewish souls perished.

Among those Jews who had escaped across the Vistula River a terrible plague broke out. They cast their dead on the cemetery in the darkness of the night, so that their unfriendly neighbors might not notice them and delight when they beheld a new grave. The plague was different from any other plague (God spare us). They were stricken with high fever, as a result of the trying journey and the fright. Many poor people whom the Gentiles did not permit entry in their homes had to sleep in the streets and they died of starvation and exposure. No man offered aid to his brother, and no father took pity on his child. More than one hundred thousand Jews perished of this disease (may the Lord preserve and save us). And the Jews became impoverished. The balance of silver and gold and garments which they managed to retain, they sold for half their value, silk and other garments, for one third of the value. Books were worthless, for there was no buyer. The Torah lay in a deserted corner, for the Gentiles bought only silver and gold and garments.

When the Jews heard that the enemies returned home, and that the nobles were following their example and were also returning to their homes and to their estates, they, too, made their way back to all those places where Polish nobles were present—up to the city of Zaslaw. From there eastward, there was not to be found at that time a single nobleman or Jew. For all those places were still occupied by many scoundrels and the nobles were afraid to travel there. Approximately two thousand soldiers, remnants of the forces of Duke Dominik, and of Duke Korecki, were in charge of Ostrog, Zaslaw and Korec. The Jews there placed their trust first in God and then in them, thinking that they might find refuge for themselves and their families. They also hoped that the townspeople would repay them the debts they owed them.

XV

THE SECOND MASSACRE OF OSTROG

The townspeople of Ostrog dealt slyly with the Jews. At first they were kind to them. They wrote to the Jews of the surrounding places who had been inhabitants of Ostrog, inviting them to return, not to fear the Cossacks, because the King had made peace with them. The poor Jews rejoiced exceedingly, believing that this was the truth. Some three hundred persons returned to Ostrog. After tarrying there three weeks, from the first of Adar to Tuesday, the eighteenth of Adar, '409,[1] the townspeople informed the Cossacks in the vicinity, to hasten there because many Jews and nobles were in their midst, and they assured them of their aid against the nobles and the Jews.

And it came to pass at midnight of the 19th of the aforementioned month of Adar, that many thousands of Cossacks came into the city of Ostrog and slew all the nobles and the Jews in their beds. Only three Jews and one officer of the nobles with eighty of his troops escaped. The Cossacks pursued them, and the nobles continued to flee ahead of them until several thousand Ukrainians had followed them from the city. Then the nobles turned their faces toward their pursuers and killed many among them, leaving only a few who escaped into the city.

When the nobles and the Jews of Zaslaw, and of the other communities near Ostrog heard of this they fled for their lives. Some escaped to Great Dubno and Olyka, and others to Krzemieniec.

And it came to pass that King Casimir, may his glory increase, and the princes heard that the Ukrainians were still rebellious, that he appointed as general, Prince Firley and equipped him with an army of thirty thousand men to wage war against the Ukrainians. General Firley, together with his army, attacked the city of Ostrog and avenged himself upon the people of the city and wrought among them great judgments.

From there he proceeded to the city of Zaslaw where he waged a great battle against the Ukrainians, near the new place of the city of Zaslaw, adjacent to the fortress, and he wrought many vengeful deeds among the people of the city. Several hundred Jewish men of strength, of the poor folk, joined him and they also proceeded to avenge themselves on their enemies. General Firley also sent a detachment of several thousand Polish troops and several hundred Jews to the neighboring places where some of the rebelling Ukrainians were still to be found, and they waged war against them and inflicted heavy losses upon them, and captured all the cities. They succeeded in all their efforts. Also Lanckoronski, the Voyevoda of Kamieniec, a great warrior, together with several thousand seasoned troops, took command of the city of Ozogowce, nine miles from Zaslaw. And he too, inflicted a heavy blow upon the Ukrainians, from another side. Throughout their encounter at Zaslaw they were victorious. The battle lasted twelve weeks and they wrought great vengeance upon the Ukrainians. As the Ukrainians had done, so were they repaid.

General Firley and his army travelled on from Zaslaw to join with Voyevoda Lanckoronski and his army, and he and all his army journeyed to the city of Czehanski Kamien. There, Lanckoronski and his army joined him, and they prepared for a major battle.[2]

When Chmiel heard that the Poles had made war upon him, and that they had devastated many Ukrainian cities and inflicted great blows upon them, he bided his time for about three months. In the interim he assembled all his troops and invited the Tartar King and army to join him.

When General Firley heard that the Ukrainians and the Tartars were mobilizing for the third time, he sent letters to King Casimir, may his glory increase, to issue a decree throughout the Kingdom of Poland, that all nobles must enlist to aid their brethren in the war. The King complied and announced throughout the provinces of his Kingdom: "All officers whose names appear in the Royal Registry must either themselves go to war, or send their servants in their place. Failure to comply with the King's decree will result in the loss of rank." And the princes were slow with their vehicles, as was their habit, while the Tartars and Ukrainians, who were many, like the sand of the sea, marched with dispatch. As the Ukrainians approached the Polish army, the Poles moved six more miles to the cities of Burmucz and Zbaraz. There Duke

Wiśniowiecki and his brother-in-law, the General Choronzhy [3] together with several thousand veteran soldiers from Lwow, joined them. And the Polish army prepared for battle in the city of Zbaraz. They fortified the city strongly and they made water obstacles all around the city.

And it came to pass on the New Moon of the Month of Ab '409, that Czar Khan, the King of the Tartars, together with a multitude of people, like the sand of the sea, and the oppressor Chmiel, and his Ukrainian people, also, a large multitude, like the sand of the sea, encircled the Polish army from a distance and besieged it. They were unable to come close to the camp because of the persistent cannon fire from the wall of the fort, which killed among them in the tens of thousands. Thus the siege on the Polish army lasted seven weeks and many nobles died of starvation. Also General Firley died in this engagement.

Duke Wiśniowiecki however strengthened the hearts of the people by deceiving them with false messages, supposedly written by the King, that he and a large army of Poles were coming to his aid. But this never happened. For no one ever left the camp, nor did anyone enter it. He did this only to encourage the people. Were it not for this they would have surrendered to the enemy, because of the severe hunger in the Polish camp. They ate the horses and the dogs because of the hunger. Occasionally Duke Wiśniowiecki and his brother-in-law, the Choronzhy with their armies, would leave their fort through a tunnel which they had dug, and attack the Ukrainian and the Tartar

MASSACRES OF OSTROG

army suddenly, killing tens of thousands. The Duke marched at the head of his men to encourage them so that their hearts would not become faint.

When King Casimir, may his glory increase, heard that the Polish army was in distress and besieged by the Ukrainians and the Tartars, he made ready his chariot, and the King himself in his glory, together with twenty thousand seasoned troops, went to war. All the nobles of Poland mobilized to follow him. But he did not wait for them and marched with his twenty thousand to aid his people in distress.

When the king came near the besieging Ukrainians and Tartars, several hundred thousand of them encircled him and his army. And the whole Polish army trembled and their hearts melted within them, and not one of them dared to unsheathe his sword. "And the King looked this way and that way and when he saw that there was no man brave to fight" [4] he was very wroth at his people and his anger burned in him.[5] And the Tartars almost captured the King alive. When the King saw that there was evil determined against him,[6] he decided to turn with his army toward the city of Zborow. And the King said to his people: "Let us escape thither; it is small and nearby and we shall be saved." [7] The King and his army found refuge there, and he waged a battle against the Ukrainians and the Tartars from the city of Zborow for about two days. In the interim the King sent forth his aide, the Nobleman Ossolinski, to the Tartar King to compromise with him and to make peace, then the oppressor Chmiel would be compelled to give his consent. The fight against the King ceased immediately and Czar Khan, the King of the Tartars, together with several hundred of his men, proceeded to the city of Zborow to speak with the King personally and to discuss with him the terms of the truce. They agreed that the King, may his glory increase, pay him two hundred thousand gold pieces, a debt due him by a previous agreement, which stipulated that a definite sum annually be paid to him as a tribute, but by which the King failed to abide. Another condition agreed upon was that the two generals in the Czar's custody be returned to the King for a ransom of one hundred thousand gold pieces. The King let him have several high ranking Polish nobles as surety, until the money will be paid.

When the oppressor, Chmiel heard that the Tartars made a truce with the King he became fearful for his life and he also went to the city of Zborow and he fell at the King's feet, and with tears beseeched him saying: "All that he had perpetrated was caused by the nobles themselves." He discussed many matters which have never been revealed to any man. But the King was too proud to converse with him, and he spoke through an interpreter. He finally compromised with him that he and his army return home, and that the King would then send five high ranking officers as commissioners to discuss the terms of the truce between the Ukrainians and the Polish people. For Chmiel had requested that thirty thousand Cossacks be exempt from taxes, as in the past; and that he should have the right to select these thirty thousand from any of the provinces that will please him, be they from those which are under the King's rule or from those which are under the rule of the nobles, and that the city of Czehiryn and its environs shall belong to him and to his seed after him, forever; also, that one of the Cossack leaders shall be one of the seven Voyevodas selected to serve in the King's Assembly; and that the King should order the Jews not to take up residence in those places where any of these thirty thousand Cossacks will reside; and many other conditions which were beyond consideration. But the King persuaded him this time to return to his home and that the five commissioners would negotiate with him.

And it came to pass after these things that the Tartars and the Ukrainians returned home. On the way, the Tartars wrought great vengeance on the Ukrainians, in the towns and in the villages, which had rebelled against the King. Some people report that the King had given them permission to destroy those places which harbored rebels. They set fire to the city of Ostrog and its environs, to Zaslaw and its environs, to Krzemieniec and its environs, to Bazilia and its environs, and to the city of Satanow and its environs up to Kamieniec-Podolski. All cities over a distance of twenty square miles were devastated and burned, and of its Ukrainian inhabitants, some were slain by the sword, and tens of thousands were taken captive by the Tartars. Only those who hid in the woods and in the swamps remained alive. And the Lord avenged on them the vengeance of the people of Israel. They themselves accepted it as a just punishment. And the land had respite from war the whole year of '410, and the year '411, according to the minor reckoning, until the feast of Passover.[8]

After the feast of Tabernacles, '410,[9] according to the minor reckoning, the Polish nobles returned to their homes and to their estates. Also the remnant of Israel, "orphans of orphans" returned. They were destitute and poor, and they found no respite even there because prices were high and food was scarce. For, of the Ukrainian people, thousands and tens of thousands perished from starvation. And the famine for bread was not so great as the lack of money. For the Cossacks and the Tartars had robbed them of all their money and treasures. Of the wealthy Ukrainians, some fled across the Dnieper, because they feared the retribution of the nobles, while others buried their money and pretended poverty. The wretched Jews, however, though indigent and destitute, appeared in the eyes of the multitude and of the nobles as rich people. And everyone cried: "Give, give." The King and the nobles demanded taxes and the Jews were penniless, and they were compelled to give a portion of what was left to them in silver and gold and clothing. They would give it away for half the value. Then came additional levies, such as the maintenance of the army and the like. They were compelled to give exorbitant tithes, so that nothing remained in their hands, and their poverty grew worse from day to day.

Nevertheless, they offered praise and thanks to the Holy One, Blessed be He, for the peace which they enjoyed. In those places where the Cossacks dwelt, business was good, for all of them were wealthy as a result of the loot of the Jews and the nobles. But no Jew or noble was permitted to reside there until the compromise had taken effect. They were permitted to establish residence only up to and including the city of Pawolocz and no further. The Cossacks were in control over a stretch of one hundred miles square of the land of [Little] Russia as a security, pending the aforementioned settlement with the nobles.

In those days, the King, may his glory increase, issued an ordinance throughout the provinces of his kingdom, that whoever had been forced to change his faith, may return to his former faith. All the forced converts returned to Judaism, and the Jews continued to reside in all the cities where they had been converted. The Jews now publicly professed their religion in those places where Jews dwelt, and in the places where the Cossacks resided, and where no Jews lived at this time, the forced converts fled, in accordance with the decree of the King. Also the women whom the Cossacks married by force, fled to the cities which were populated by Jews. Thus hundreds of forced converts became Jews again. In the places where severe carnage took place, hundreds of boys and girls and infants, had been converted. The Jews took them back by force from the hands of the Gentiles. After thorough investigation, they provided them with identifying tags giving the names of the families to which they belonged. These were hung on the neck of each child. Many women had become Agunoth,[10] and many widows who had become subject to levirate marriage [11] became Agunoth because the levir had departed from the land. The authorities of the Council of Four Lands,[12] may the Rock and Redeemer preserve them, instituted many appropriate ordinances for their benefit and they instituted a public fast for the whole Kingdom of Poland, to be observed on the twentieth day of Sivan, for generations to come. For on that day the terrible slaughter of Nemirow had occurred, and it had been the first community to submit to the massacre, for the glorification of His Name, may the merit of its martyrs stand us in good stead, and may the Lord avenge their blood.

After these things the King elevated Duke Wiśniowiecki above the other nobles and appointed him Supreme General over the whole Polish army. But he would not accept the appointment unless the honor would be for life. Should the two generals, now held captive by the Tartars, return, they would not replace him in this capacity. Only then would he lead the Polish army beyond the River Dnieper and subjugate the Cossacks, with the help of God, so that everyone would be enabled to return to his possession.

When Chmiel heard of this thing, he feared for his life, lest the King grant his request, for the hearts of all the people were with Duke Wiśniowiecki. He immediately sent a message to the Tartar King to release the two Polish generals from the dungeon; that he would pay the balance of the ransom money due him. Chmiel did this not because of his love for them, but because of his hatred for Duke Wiśniowiecki, to prevent him from becoming the supreme general. The

MASSACRES OF OSTROG

King of the Tartars thus released the two generals, Potocki and Kalinowsky. The Polish King and his nobles were surprised at the release of the two generals by the King of the Tartars, and they knew not the cause thereof. The King restored them to their former offices.

In those days the oppressor, Chmiel, together with all his army, attacked the provinces of Wallachia and destroyed them because they sheltered many nobles and Jews and because the Wallachians acquired from the Tartars by force hundreds of captives and gave them their freedom. Upon their return from the provinces of Wallachia they brought with them a vast amount of booty and sold much of it to the Jews. But no Jew suffered injury this time because there was peace with the Jews.

In those days the Russians in the province of Moscowy also rebelled against the King of Poland. They were joined by a host of riffraff from the Cossacks. The oppressor Chmiel wrote letters to the King not to fear the Moscovite rebellion; that he and his Cossacks would march upon them, engage them in battle and make them subject to the King. But the King in his wisdom understood that Chmiel was merely seeking a pretext and he was compelled to make peace with the Moscovites.

In those days the King of Poland sent a commission of high ranking nobles to make a settlement with the Cossacks but it was unsuccessful. For the Cossacks made many demands which could not be met by the

King and the nobles, and the matter was delayed until the festival of Passover '411, according to the minor reckoning.

And it came to pass prior to the aforementioned Passover that the Tartars and the Ukrainians assembled a fourth time, and on that Passover, the children of Israel drank the "four cups of poison." They slew hundreds of Jews, and hundreds went into captivity to the Tartars. The latter day troubles make one oblivious of those of the past. "And Jacob fled" for the fourth time, and all the children of Israel escaped to the Metropolis of Lwow. And the King himself, may his glory increase, went to fight against them, and with him were three hundred thousand able soldiers of the Polish army, and eighty thousand men composed of Germans, French, and Spanish soldiers, also one thousand Jewish fighters. Three hundred thousand Poles were stationed near Lublin so that the Polish people would not be in one mass, because of the famine. Since the day the Kingdom of Poland was founded unto the present, there were not so many Polish troops gathered together as in those days. The Tartars and the Ukrainians also comprised a vast throng, like the sand of the sea, that cannot be counted for multitude.

The King prepared for a great battle, and he pitched his tent in the Monastery in the city of Sokal, and the rest of the King's army readied itself for battle between the city of Sokal and the city of Beresteczko, and with them were the two generals and Duke Wiśniowiecki. The Tartars and the Ukrainians came upon them suddenly with their accustomed shouts and savage outcries and said: "Let us attack the Polish people and we will defeat them as we did in our previous attempts." And they knew not that God was with us and with the King, may his glory increase. At first they succeeded and inflicted a blow on the Polish army. But afterwards the hand of the Polish army prevailed and, reinforced by the Germans, they girded themselves with strength, and they struck a severe blow on the Tartars and Ukrainians, and they smote them and pursued them unto destruction. The Tartar King escaped to his land in great embarrassment and with very few of his forces. He took the oppressor Chmiel with him into captivity, because the latter did not inform him of the strength of the King's army, and caused him the embarrassment of being compelled to escape with only a small number of his troops, and to lose most of his forces. All the high ranking officers, among them the nephew of the Tartar King, became the prisoners of the King. The remaining Cossack forces were besieged by the Polish forces for many days. They arose and escaped in the evening, leaving their tents, and horses and carts filled with everything good, the whole camp intact, and they fled for their lives. The King, may his glory increase, together with his nobles and followers, returned to their homes, with great rejoicing and with happy hearts on the seventeenth of Ab, '411, according to the minor reckoning. And the Tartar King sent letters to the King, may his glory increase, to release his nephew in exchange of his foe, the oppressor, who at this time had been his prisoner; he would also return four thousand high ranking Polish nobles, now in his captivity. But the King refused. He replied with pride to the Tartar King that he may retain the oppressor Chmiel for the present and that he intended to take him later by force. This the King said to impress upon the Tartar King that he and his people intend to make war upon the Tartars. Then the King sent his two generals and Duke Wiśniowiecki, and, with them, one hundred and fifty thousand able bodied warriors, to conquer all the Ukrainian cities in the land of [Little] Russia, and to make war on the Tartars afterwards. This they did. They proceeded and captured the cities in the Land of [Little] Russia one by one.

At this time the nobles became envious of Duke Wiśniowiecki, who had been rising in popularity, and they handed him a deadly poison to drink and Duke Wiśniowiecki died. May his memory be a blessing. He left behind him a sixteen-year-old son who was also an able warrior, and he took his father's place. And it came to pass that the King of the Tartars heard that the hero, the Duke, died and that two generals were preparing to make war on him, he made peace with the oppressor Chmiel. Chmiel paid him a ransom of eighteen million gold pieces, and also supported him. The Tartars and the Ukrainians assembled in a vast multitude, like the sand of the sea, a fifth time, to make war against Poland. The great war thus renewed itself in Poland after the Holy Days, '412, according to the minor reckoning and the war has been continuing to the present day.[13] Sometimes the enemy prevails, and sometimes, the King prevails. The children of Israel however, are becoming poorer and poorer. Moreover, a severe epidemic has broken out in the whole Kingdom of Poland. In the city of Cracow, and in other communities, in the Kingdom of Poland, in the summer of '412, according to the minor reckoning, more than twenty thousand persons perished. May the Lord have mercy upon them. Unto the present day throughout the Kingdom of Poland, there reigns the sword, famine and a great pestilence. And these latter troubles make us forget the former. Every day the tragedy is greater than on the day preceeding it. "In the evening they would say; would it were morning, and in the morning they would say; would it were evening." [14] And the verses: "Also every sickness, and every plague, which is not written in the book of the law, etc . . . And the Lord shall scatter thee among all the peoples, from one end of the earth even unto the other end of the earth," [15] have come to pass. What can we say, what can we speak, or how can we justify ourselves? Shall we say we have not sinned? Behold, our iniquities testify against us. For we have sinned, and the Lord found out the iniquity of his servants. Would the Holy One, blessed be He, dispense judgment without justice? But we may say that "He whom God loveth he chastiseth." [16] We may also apply to them the verse: "And begin at my sanctuary." [17] Read not Mimikdoshi (from my sanctuary), but read Mimkudoshai (from my sanctified).[18] For since the day the Holy Temple was destroyed the righteous are seized by death for the iniquities of the generation.

XVI

THE INNER LIFE OF THE JEWS IN THE KINGDOM OF POLAND

And now I will begin to describe the practices of the Jews in the Kingdom of Poland, which were founded on principles of righteousness and steadfastness.

It is said in Tractate Aboth: Simon the Just was one of the last survivors of the Great Synagogue. He used to say: "Upon three things the world is based: Upon the Torah, upon divine service, and upon the practice of charity." [1] Rabban Simeon, the son of Gamaliel said: "By three things is the world preserved: by truth, by judgment and by peace." [2] All the six pillars upon which the world rests were in existence in the Kingdom of Poland.

The Pillar of the Torah: Matters that are well known need no proof, for throughout the dispersions of Israel there was nowhere so much learning as in the Kingdom of Poland. Each community maintained academies, and the head of each academy was given an ample salary so that he could maintain his school without worry, and that the study of the Torah might be his sole occupation. The head of the academy did not leave his house the whole year except to go from

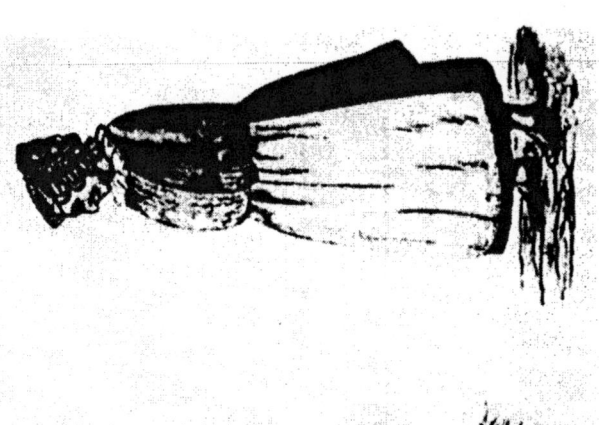

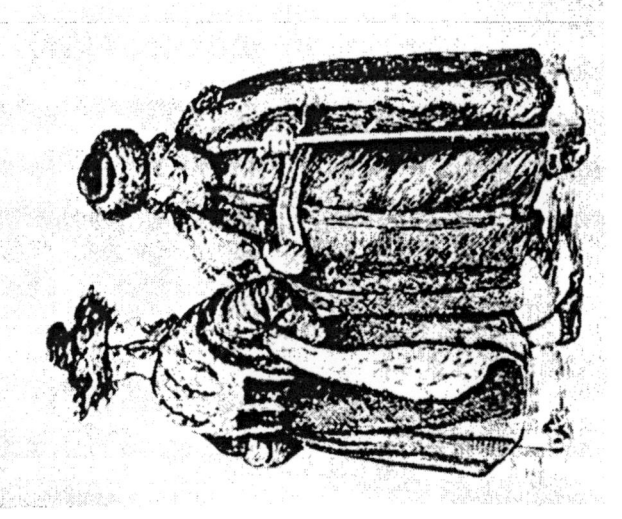

TYPICAL CLOTHES OF POLISH JEWS
DURING 16TH AND 17TH CENTURIES

SABBATH ATTIRE FOR WOMEN

the house of study to the synagogue. Thus he was engaged in the study of the Torah day and night. Each community maintained young men and provided for them a weekly allowance of money that they might study with the head of the academy. And for each young man they also maintained two boys to study under his guidance, so that he would orally discuss the Gemara (Talmud), the commentaries of Rashi, and the Tosafoth, which he had learned, and thus he would gain experience in the subtlety of Talmudic argumentation. The boys were provided with food from the community benevolent fund or from the public kitchen. If the community consisted of fifty householders it supported not less than thirty young men and boys. One young man and two boys would be assigned to one householder. And the young man ate at his table as one of his sons. Although the young man received a stipend from the community, the householder provided him with all the food and drink that he needed. Some of the more charitable householders also allowed the boys to eat at their table, thus three persons would be provided with food and drink by one householder the entire year.

There was scarcely a house in all the Kingdom of Poland where its members did not occupy themselves with the study of the Torah. Either the head of the family was himself a scholar, or else his son, or his son-in-law studied, or one of the young men eating at his table. At times, all of these were to be found in one house. Thus they realized all the three things of which Raba spoke in Tractate Sabbath, chapter I: Raba said:

"He who loves the Rabbis will have sons who are Rabbis; he who honors the Rabbis will have Rabbis for sons-in-law; he who stands in awe of the Rabbis will himself be a Rabbinical scholar." [3] Thus there were many scholars in every community. A community of fifty householders had twenty scholars who achieved the title Morenu or Haver.[4] The head of the academy was above all these, and the scholars were submissive to him and they would go to his academy to attend his discourses.

The program of study in the Kingdom of Poland was as follows: The term of study consisted of the period which required the young men and the boys to study with the head of the academy in the academy. In the summer it extended from the first day of the month of Iyar till the fifteenth day of the month Ab, and in the winter, from the first day of the month of Cheshvan, till the fifteenth day of the month of Shevat. After the fifteenth of Shevat or the fifteenth of Ab, the young men and the boys were free to study wherever they preferred. From the first day of Iyar till the Feast of Weeks, and in the winter from the first day of Cheshvan till Chanukkah, all the students of the academy studied Gemara, the commentaries of Rashi and Tsoafoth, with great diligence. Each day they studied a halachah —one page of Gemara with the commentaries of Rashi and Tosafoth is called a halachah.

All the scholars and the young students of the community as well as all those who showed inclination to study the Torah assembled in the academy. The head of the academy alone occupied a chair and the scholars and the other students stood about him. Before the head of the academy appeared they would engage in a discussion of the Law, and when he arrived each one would ask him that which he found difficult in the Law and he would offer his explanation to each of them.

They were all silent, as the head of the academy delivered his lecture and presented the new results of his study. After discussing his new interpretations the head of the academy would discuss a chilluk (a difference in the point of view of two authorities), which proceeded in the following manner: He would cite a contradiction from the Gemara, or Rashi, or Tosafoth, he would question deletions and pose contradictory statements and provide solutions which would also prove perplexing; and then he would propose solutions until the Law was completely clarified.

In the summer they would not leave the academy before noon. From the Feast of Weeks till the New Year, and from Chanukkah till Passover, the head of the academy would not engage in so many discussions. He would study with the scholars the Codes such as the Arbaah Turim [5] (the Four Rows) and their commentaries. With young men he would study Rav Alfas [6] and other works. In any case, they also studied Gemara, Rashi, and Tosafoth, till the first day of Ab or the fifteenth day of Shevat. From then on until Passover or the New Year they studied the codes and similar works only. Some weeks prior to the fifteenth day of Ab or the fifteenth day of Shevat, the head of the academy would honor each student to lead in the discussions in his stead. The honor was given both to the scholars and the students. They would present the discussion, and the head of the academy would listen and then join in the disputation. This was done to exercise their intellect. The same tractate was studied throughout the Kingdom of Poland in the proper sequence of the Six Orders.[7]

Each head of an academy had one inspector who daily went from school to school to look after the boys, both rich and poor, that they should study. He would warn them every day in the week that they should study and not loiter in the streets. On Thursdays all the boys had to be examined by the superintendent on what they had learned during the week, and he who knew nothing of what he had studied or erred in one thing was flogged by the inspector at the command of the director, and was otherwise also chastised before the boys so that he should remember to study more diligently the following week. Likewise on Sabbath Eve all the boys went in a group to the head of the academy to be questioned on what they had learned during the week, as in the aforementioned procedure. In this manner there was fear upon the boys and they studied with regularity. Also during the Shelosheth Yemei Hagbalah (the three days preceding the Feast of Weeks) and during Chanukkah, the young men and the boys were obliged to review what they had studied during that term, and for this the community leaders gave specified gifts of money. Such was the practice till the fifteenth of Ab or the fifteenth of Shevat. After that the head of the academy, together with all his students, the young men and the boys, journeyed to the fair. In the summer they travelled to the fair of Zaslaw and to the fair of Jaroslaw; in the winter to the fairs of Lwow and Lublin. There the young men and boys were free to study in any academy they preferred. Thus at each of the fairs hundreds of academy heads, thousands of young men, and tens of thousands of boys, and Jewish merchants, and Gentiles like the sand on the shore of the sea, would gather. For people would come to the fair from one end of the world to the other. Whoever had a son or daughter of marriageable age went to the fair and there arranged a match. For there was ample opportunity for everyone to find his like and his mate. Thus hundreds and sometimes thousands of such matches would be arranged at each fair. And Jews, both men and women, walked about the fair, dressed in royal garments. For they were held in esteem in the eyes of the rulers and in the eyes of the Gentiles, and the children of Israel were many like the sand of the sea, but now, because of our sins, they have become few. May the Lord have mercy upon them.

In each community great honor was accorded to the head of the academy. His words were heard by rich and poor alike. None questioned his authority. Without him no one raised his hand or foot, and as he commanded so it came to be. In his hand he carried a stick, and a lash, to smite and to flog, to punish and to chastise transgressors, to institute ordinances, to establish safeguards, and to declare the forbidden. Nevertheless everyone loved the head of the academy, and he that had a good portion such as fatted fowl, or capons or good fish, would honor the head of the academy, with half or all, and with other gifts of silver and gold without measure. In the synagogue, too, most of those who bought honors would accord them to the head of the academy. It was obligatory to call him to the Torah reading third, on the Sabbath and the first days of the Festivals. And if the head of the academy happened to be a Cohen or a Levite, he would be given preference despite the fact that there may have been others entitled to the honor of Cohen or Levi, or the concluding portion. No one left the synagogue on the Sabbath or the Festival until the head of the academy walked out first and his pupils after him, and then the whole congregation accompanied him to his home. On the Festivals the entire congregation followed him to his house to greet him. For this reason all the scholars were envious and studied with diligence, so that they too, might advance to this state, and become an academy head in some community, and out of doing good with an ulterior motive, there comes the doing good for its own sake, and the land was filled with knowledge.

The Pillar of Divine Service: At this time prayer has replaced (sacrificial) service, as it is written: "So we will render for bullocks, the offering of our lips." [8] Prayers were "set upon sockets of fine gold." At the head was the fellowship of those who rose before dawn, called "Shomrim La Boker," "they that watch for the morning," [9] to pray and to mourn over the destruction of the Temple. With the coming of dawn the members of the Chevra Tehillim would rise to recite Psalms for about an hour before prayers. Each week they would complete the recitation of the entire Book of Psalms.

And far be it, that any man should oversleep the time of prayer in the morning and not go to the synagogue, except for unusual circumstances. When a man went to the synagogue, he would not depart thence to his business until he had heard some words of the Law expounded by a scholar or a passage from the commentary of Rashi on the Torah, the Prophets, the Hagiographa, the Mishnah or some laws of ritual, whatever his heart desired to learn; for in all synagogues there were many groups of scholars who taught others in the synagogue immediately after evening and morning prayers. They would observe: "They shall go from strength to strength, every one of them appeareth before God in Zion." [10]

The Pillar of Charity: There was no measure for the dispensation of charity in the Kingdom of Poland, especially as regards hospitality. If a scholar or preacher visited a community, even one which had a system of issuing communal tickets [11] to be offered hospitality by a householder, he did not have to humiliate himself to obtain a ticket, but went to some community leader and stayed wherever he pleased. The community beadle then came and took his credentials to collect funds to show it to the synagogue official or the community leader for the month, and they gave an appropriate gift which was delivered by the beadle in dignified manner. He was then the guest of the householder for as many days as he desired. Similarly all other transients who received tickets, would be the guests of a householder, whose turn it was by lot, for as many days as he wished. A ticket was good for at least three days. The guest was given food and drink, morning, noon and evening. If they wished to depart they would be given provisions for the road, and they would be conveyed by horse and carriage from one community to another. If young men or boys or older men or unmarried girls, came from distant places, they would be forthwith furnished with garments. Those who wanted to work at a trade would be apprenticed to a tradesman, and those who wanted to be servants in a house would be assigned to serve in a house. Those who wanted to study would be provided with a teacher, and afterwards, when he became an important young man, a rich man would take him to his house and give him his daughter in marriage as well as several thousand gold pieces for a dowry, and he would clothe him in royal garments—for who is royalty? The scholars.[12] After the wedding he would send him away from his home to study in great academies. When he returned home after two or three years, his father-in-law would maintain an academy for him in his home and he would spend much money among the householders who were prominent scholars that they should attend his academy for a number of years, until he also will become a head of an academy in some community. Even if the lad was not yet an important student at that time but had a desire to study, enabling him to become a scholar after he had studied, there would at times come a rich man who had a young daughter, and give him food and drink and clothes, and all his needs, as he would to his own son, and he would hire a teacher for him until he was ready with his studies, then he would

INNER LIFE OF JEWS IN POLAND 119

give him his daughter in marriage. There is no greater benevolence than this. Similarly there were very praiseworthy regulations for poor unmarried girls in every province. No poor girl reached the age of eighteen without being married, and many pious women devoted themselves to this worthy deed. May the Lord recompense them and have compassion upon the remnant of Israel.

The Pillar of Justice was in the Kingdom of Poland as it was in Jerusalem before the destruction of the Temple, when courts were set up in every city, and if one refused to be judged by the court of his city he went to the nearest court, and if he refused to be judged by the nearest court, he went before the great court. For in every province there was a great court. Thus in the capital city of Ostrog there was the great court for Volhynia and the Ukraine, and in the capital city of Lwow there was the great court for [Little] Russia. There were thus many communities each of which had a great court for its own province.

If two important communities had a dispute between them, they would let themselves be judged by the heads of the council of Four Lands [18] (may their Rock and Redeemer preserve them) who would be in session twice a year. One leader would be chosen from each important community, added to these, were six great scholars from the land of Poland, and these were known as the Council of Four Lands. They would be in session during every fair in Lublin between Purim and Passover, and during every fair at Jaroslaw in the month of Ab or Elul. The leaders of the Four Lands were like the Sanhedrin in the Chamber of Hewn Stones.[14] They had the authority to judge all Israel in the Kingdom of Poland, to establish safeguards, to institute ordinances, and to punish each man as they saw fit. Each difficult matter was brought before them and they judged it. And the leaders of the Four Lands selected judges from the provinces to relieve their burden, and these were called judges of the provinces. They attended to cases involving money matters. Fines, titles, and other difficult laws were brought before the leaders of the Four Lands, may their Rock and Redeemer preserve them. Never was a dispute among Jews brought before a Gentile judge or before a nobleman, or before the King, may his glory increase, and if a Jew took his case before a Gentile court he was punished and chastised severely, to observe: "Even our enemies themselves being judges." [15]

The Pillar of Truth: Every community appointed men in charge of weights and measures, and of other business dealings, so that everything would be conducted according to truth and trustworthiness.

The Pillar of Peace: For it is said: "The Lord will give strength unto His people; the Lord will bless His people with peace." There was in Poland so much interest in learning that no three people sat down to a meal without discussing the words of Torah, for throughout the repast everyone indulged in debating matters of the Law and puzzling passages in the Midrashim, in order to observe: "Thy law is in my inmost parts." [16] And the Holy One blessed be He, recompensed them so that even when they were in the land of their enemies, He did not despise them and did not break his covenant with them. And wherever their feet trod the ground among our brothers of the House of Israel they were treated with great generosity, above all, our brethren of the House of Israel who were in distress and in captivity among the Tartars. For the Tartars led them to Constantinople, a city that was a mother in Israel, and to the famed city of Salonica, and to other communities in Turkey and Egypt, and in Barbary and other provinces of Jewish dispersion where they were ransomed for much money, as mentioned above. To this day they have not ceased to ransom prisoners that are brought to them each day. The Lord recompense them.

Those who escaped the sword of the enemy in every land where their feet trod, such as Moravia, Austria, Bohemia, Germany, Italy, were treated with kindness and were given food and drink and lodging and garments and many gifts, each according to his importance, and they also favored them with other things. Especially in Germany did they do more than they could. May their justice appear before God to shield them and all Israel wherever they are congregated, so that Israel may dwell in peace and tranquility in their habitations. May their merit be counted for us and for our children, that the Lord should hearken to our cries and gather our dispersed from the four corners of the earth, and send us our righteous Messiah, speedily in our day. Amen, Selah.

NOTES TO TRANSLATOR'S INTRODUCTION

[1] There is considerable controversy among chroniclers and historians with regard to the number of communities that were devastated and also with regard to the number slain. Rabbi Sabbathai Cohen in his brief account of the massacres records that approximately 300 communities were destroyed and a little more than 100,000 people slain. Most likely his figures represent a minimum. According to another record, 744 communities were destroyed and 650 thousand persons were slain. See Jacob Schatzki's introduction to the Yiddish translation of Yeven Metzulah, Yivo Wilno, 1938, 83 ff.

[2] Shatzky, *ibid.*, 45 ff.

[3] See Di Yidn in Ukraine by I. S. Hertz, New York, 1949, 197. Following the massacres of 1648 and 1649 a number of accusations against the Jews became current among the people which attempted to justify the slaughter. Foremost among these was the one which stated that the Jews leased Christian churches thereby offending the religious sensibilities of the Ukrainians and arousing their anger. Hertz discusses fully these accusations and concludes that they have no historical basis and that no conscientious historian will subscribe to them. They were originally written for propaganda purposes. Shatzky maintains that such procedure was quite normal in those days, and disagrees with Hertz that the accusations were unfounded. See Shatzky's article in the "Zukunft," New York, December, 1949.

[4] From the German, Hauptmann.

[5] See Hertz' Di Yidn in Ukraine, New York, 1949, 104.

[6] From the Russian word Za porogi, meaning, "beyond the Falls."

[7] The "Three Weeks" beginning with the 17th day of Tammuz and concluding with 9th day of Av are observed as a period of mourning commemorating the siege of Jerusalem and the destruction of the Temple.

[8] Hanover gives the date of the Pawliuk rebellion as 1639. Actually it started in 1637.

[9] See *Abyss of Despair*, p. 28.

[10] Shatzky's introduction to Yeven Metzulah, Yivo Wilno, 1938.

[11] Sholem Asch's Kiddush Hashem.

NOTES

AUTHOR'S INTRODUCTION

1 Lamentations 3:1.
2 Ps. 48:3.
3 Lamentations 2:2.
4 Deut. 32:9.
5 Lamentations 2:1.
6 The term Yavan, Yevanim-Greeks, Greeks is used by Hanover throughout his chronicle to identify the Ukrainians who were followers of the Greek Orthodox Church.
7 Zoth is numerically equal to 408, namely, the year 5408 of the era of Creation or 1648, of the Common Era.
8 Ps. 32:6.
9 Ps. 69:3.
10 The virus of both is fatal.
11 Aboth 1:2, Torah, worship and benevolence: Aboth 1:18, Truth, Judgment and Peace.
12 This book was never published.
13 Southeast Poland or Little Russia.

Chapter I

1 1585.
2 Sigismund III was crowned King of Poland in 1587.
3 1592.
4 The Shoot of David, a chronicle of general and Jewish interest by the renowed Jewish chronicler David Gans of Prague (1541–1613) first published in 1592.
5 Catholicism.
6 Is. 8:14.
7 Ex. 1:14.
8 The Jewish People.

Chapter II

1 1602. The date mentioned by Hanover is incorrect. This rebellion had its beginning in 1596.
2 There were two brothers Nolevaiko, one Danion, a priest and the other, Semion, a lieutenant. Apparently, the second was the rebel.
3 Gen. 22:17. Hanover is inclined to exaggerate. He makes use of this phrase whenever he wishes to convey the idea of a multitude.

The author uses the traditional reference "holy congregation" for each community, but for the sake of smoother reading the translator omitted it.

[4] In the Province of Zhitomir, Wolhynia.
[5] Judges 3:11.
[6] 1631. Hanover errs in the date of Sigismund's death. He died in April 1632.
[7] 1632. Wladislaw was elected king in Nov. 1632 and was crowned in February 1633.
[8] 1645.
[9] 1646.
[10] Louis XIV.

Chapter III

[1] 1639. Actually the rebellion started in 1637.
[2] The Dnieper Falls.
[3] Literally: "Inscribe on the horns of the ox that you have no share in the God of Israel or be killed." According to the Midrash (Lev. Rabba, 13) this ultimatum was offered to the Jews in the day of the Syrian King Antiochus Epiphanes.
[4] Proverbs 21:30.
[5] Ex. 32:24. The "calf" refers to Chmielnicki, "and the misfortune came forth."

Chapter IV

[1] 1648, 1649, 1650, 1651, 1652.
[2] 1648.
[3] West of the Dnieper.
[4] Really Chmielnicki.
[5] Proverbs 26:25.
[6] b. Erubin 65 a.
[7] March 9, 1648.
[8] Numbers 31:12.
[9] Numbers Rabba XX. The two had been perennial enemies but united against Israel, on its way to the Promised Land.
[10] Gen. 22:7.
[11] Numbers 13:30.
[12] May 25, 1648.
[13] b Sanhedrin 39 b.
[14] May 27, 1648.
[15] The foremost community of Volhynia.

NOTES

16 Sanhedrin b. Sanhedrin 49 b.
17 Gen. 23:6.
18 Esther 9:30.
19 Esther 8:11.
20 Esther 4:3.
21 b. Sanhedrin 72 a.
22 b. Sanhedrin 74 a.
23 Aboth 3:2.
24 b. Baba Kamma 52 a.

Chapter V

1 June 10, 1648.
2 Lamentations 5:11.
3 Author of "Shibre Luchoth" (Broken Tablets), Lublin 1680.

Chapter VI

1 Maxim Krzywonos, ruthless commander of the massacres of Tulczyn and other communities.
2 Gen. 34:25.
3 Hanover deviates from historical fact in this report. The Duke did not have any daughters.
4 Governor of the province.

Chapter VII

1 July 20, 1648.
2 p. Hagigah I. 7.
3 A Kabbalist. Some of his mystical writings were published posthumously.
4 Rabbi Isaac Luria, founder of a new trend in Jewish mysticism known as the Lurianic Kabbalah lived in Safed, Palestine, in the 16th century.
5 July 26, 1648. The Sabbath on which the first chapter of Isaiah is read in the Synagogue precedes the Fast of Ab, which commemorates the destruction of the Temple. "Hazon" is the opening word of the chapter.
6 Exodus 15:15. "Edom"—the Catholic rulers.
7 b. Moed Katan 25 b.
8 Ez. 7:19.
9 Lev. 26:17.
10 Deut. 28:65, 66.

NOTES

Chapter VIII

1 Isaiah 14:19.

Chapter IX

1 July 28, 1648.
2 The Ikwa River (?).
3 September 20, 1648.

Chapter X

1 White Russia was included in Lithuania.
2 Numbers 14:45.

Chapter XI

1 Ezekiel 21:27.
2 Koniecpolski.
3 Deut. 32:25.

Chapter XII

1 October 1648.
2 Cracow, Poznan (Posen), Lublin and Lwow (Lemberg).
3 The function of the Shtadlan was to act as intermediary and to intercede on behalf of the Jewish community before the government.

Chapter XIII

1 November 2, 1648.

Chapter XIV

1 Literally, he examined it. The procedure following ritual slaughter is to examine the entrails of the animal for symptoms of disease.
2 Gen. 26:8.
3 John Casimir was elected King of Poland at the end of 1648.

Chapter XV

1 February 13–March 2, 1649.
2 June 1649.

NOTES

³ The Banner-bearer Koniecpolski.
⁴ Ex. 2:12.
⁵ Esther 1:12.
⁶ Esther 7:7.
⁷ Gen. 19:20.
⁸ 1650–1651.
⁹ Oct. 1649.

¹⁰ Literally, bound. A woman whose husband has either abandoned her, or has not been heard from for a long time. The status of such a woman remains unchanged since there is no proof of his death. Jewish law does not admit the presumption of death from a prolonged absence, nor can a wife obtain a divorce from an absent husband.

¹¹ The marriage with the widow of a childless brother. Levir is the Latin for a husband's brother. To prevent the complete extinction of the family line, the perishing of a man's name and his property going to others, the surviving brother of a childless man was required to marry the widow and thus raise up an heir to the deceased man's name. See Deut. 25:5.

¹² The Council of Four Lands included Great Poland with its Capital, Posen, Little Poland, (Cracow), Polish or Red Russia (Podolia and Galicia, with Lemberg as the Capital), and Volhynia (Ostrog or Kremenetz as the Capital).

¹³ 1653.
¹⁴ Deut. 28:67.
¹⁵ Deut. 28:61, 62, 64.
¹⁶ Prov. 3:12.
¹⁷ Ez. 9:6.
¹⁸ Lamen. Rabbati II.

Chapter XVI

¹ Aboth 1:2.
² Aboth 1:18.
³ T.B. Sabbath 23b.

⁴ Our teacher. Haver is Associate. These were titles of distinction conferred upon Talmudic scholars.

⁵ The author is Rabbi Jacob ben Asher, died in Toledo, Spain in 1340.

⁶ Rabbi Isaac Alfasi, renowned Talmudist of Fez, North Africa, 1013–1103.

⁷ The six orders of the Mishna: Zeraim (Seeds), Moed (Seasons), Nashim (Women), Nezikin (Damages), Kodashim (Sanctities), and Tohoroth (Purities).

NOTES

8 Hosea 14:3.
9 Ps. 130:6.
10 Ps. 84:8.
11 Food tickets (Pletten) which entitled the bearer to have his meals with a householder.
12 T.B. Gittin 62a.
13 See Chap. 15, note 12.
14 One of the chambers in the Holy Temple where the Sanhedrin convened.
15 Deut. 32:31.
16 Ps. 40:9.